POEMS of the SCOTTISH HILLS

KU-241-243

POEMS
of the
SCOTTISH
HILLS

AN ANTHOLOGY
selected by
HAMISH BROWN

Foreword by
Norman MacCaig

ABERDEEN UNIVERSITY PRESS

First published 1982
published and distributed outside of North America by
Aberdeen University Press
A member of the Pergamon Group

© Introduction, selection and illustrations Hamish Brown 1982

EWART

British Library Cataloguing in Publication Data
Poems of the Scottish hills.
1. English poetry   2. Mountains—Scotland
—Poetry
I. Brown, Hamish
821'.008'036   PR1195.M/

ISBN 0 08 028476 0 (hard)
ISBN 0 08 028477 9 (flexi)

PRINTED IN GREAT BRITAIN
THE UNIVERSITY PRESS
ABERDEEN

Foreword

I've heard many people say things that were so unbelievable my jaw dropped, and the winner of the lot was this.—A half a century ago, when the flood of tourists in the remoter Highlands was a wee trickle, I was standing in front of the Post Office at Lochearnhead beside my bike (loaded with a tent and all the accompanying doldrummage—a friend's invention, that). A young fellow, with bike etc., was near-hand and we got speaking. He told me, in his English accent, that he was cutting his holiday short. It had been a splendid summer (honestly), so I asked him why. 'Was it the midges?' I said. 'No, no', he answered. 'There are no views.'

I asked him to hoist his eyelids and look straight in front of him. And he said, 'You can't see the view for these damned hills.' Never did my jaw drop further.

Of course a surprising proportion of Scots who live in our big cities are only first generation townees—as I am—and the smaller towns have the countryside at their back doors. It's the most natural thing in the world, come the holidays, to make a bee-line for the mountains and the waters that add to them their own special beauties. Not that I despise the pleasures of the city. Now that I'm, well, getting on and am not so swack as I used to be, I think my ideal life would be to spend the six winter months in the city and the other six in the Highlands—particularly the North West and, even more particularly, the Gairloch to Kinlochbervie bit of it.

There's a reason for this. I'm not a mountaineer, I'm a fisherman. I understand what makes a man a collector of Munros, but, though I've been on the tops of a good many of them, I'm happy enough to be *among* mountains, inveigled onwards by a loch I've never visited. If there's a loch in a corrie I'll go there. And a reason why I love that particular area is that it's scattered with an inexhaustible number of lochs and lochans. Another reason is that the mountains there, though most of them aren't Munros at all, stand separate from each other, which makes them seem higher than they really are. For, wild wilderness though it is, in a sense it's a small-scale landscape. This has a happy result. In, say, the Cairngorms, you've to walk a fair good bit to make an appreciable change in what you're looking at: up there, a half mile will do.

Anyway, there's more to a mountain than the cairn on top of it: the countless experiences offered to your feet, your five senses and your muscles and—I'm trying to avoid the word, but I can't—a feeling of freedom, of dealing with the natural, physical world, obeying its natural laws—savage enough, some of them, till you compare them with the worse perversions of the blessed intelligence of men.

Footnote: I mentioned my favourite corner of Scotland. You'll all have your own. And, though I doubt if J. C. Milne fundamentally meant it, my heart leapt up when I read his wee poem, *The patriot*:

> Fecht for Britain? Hoot awa!
> For Bonnie Scotland? Imphm, man, na!
> For Lochnagar? Wi' clook and claw!

NORMAN MacCAIG

Contents

FOREWORD *Norman MacCaig*   v

INTRODUCTION   xiii

QUESTIONS AND ANSWERS

Scotland Small? *Hugh MacDiarmid*   3
In the Highlands *Robert Louis Stevenson*   3
Older Now *Dave Gingell*   4
Last Journey *John Davidson*   4
The Peak *Wilfred Gibson*   5
Highland Loves *Rennie McOwan*   6
Rock, Be My Dream *MacKnight Black*   7
Freedom of the Hills *Douglas Fraser*   7
Owre the Hills *William Soutar*   8
The Spell o' the Hills *Douglas Fraser*   8
And Happy Am I *Syd Scroggie*   9
Wine o Living *Matt Marshall*   10
The Kingship of the Hills *W H Ogilive*   11
At Euston *A M Harbord*   11
I Leave Tonight from Euston *Anon*   12
For Tony, Dougal, Mick, Bugs, Nick, et al *Dave Bathgate*   13
Of Only a Single Poem *G J F Dutton*   14
O Aa the Manly Sports *J K Annand*   14
Three Girls on a Buttress *Eilidh Nisbet*   15
Pitch Seven *Hamish Brown*   16
Rock Leader *Dave Bathgate*   17
The Climber Surveys His Mountain *Hugh Ouston*   18
Magma *G J F Dutton*   18
On Falling *Andrew Greig*   19
The Climbing Rope *A V Stuart*   20
In Memoriam *Dave Gingell*   21
On a Ledge *William Bell*   21
NN 616410 *Bill Tulloch*   23
One Way Down *David Craig*   24
On Walking Back to the Bus *Alan Gardner*   24
On Looking at an Old Climbing Photograph *Douglas Fraser*   25
Hills of the Middle Distance *Archie Mitchell*   25
A Song of Degrees *W P Ker*   26
The Quiet Glen *Douglas Fraser*   26
Silver in the Wind *Ian Strachan*   27

The Dipper *Phoebe Hesketh* 27
The Hooded Crow *Rennie McOwan* 28
The Echoing Cliff *Andrew Young* 29
Eagles and Isles *Wilfrid W Gibson* 29
The Eagle *Andrew Young* 29
Buzzard *Michael Daugherty* 30
The Rowan *Violet Jacob* 30
Moorburn in Spring *Anon* 31
In the Rut *Hamish Brown* 32
Stags *William Montgomerie* 33
Death of a Hind *Alasdair Maclean* 33
The Ice has Spoken *Denis Rixson* 34
Mountain Sculpture *James Will* 35
Stanes *Duncan Glen* 36
Bog *Leen Volwerk* 36
Mist *Andrew Young* 37
Mist *Gill Mann* 37
Kythans *Stewart McGavin* 38
Clouds and Clay *Valerie Gillies* 39
February Thaw *G J F Dutton* 39
Spate in Winter Midnight *Norman MacCaig* 40
View From My Window *Alasdair Maclean* 40
A Hint o' Snaw *William Soutar* 41
Discomfort in High Places *Sydney Tremayne* 41
Night Up There *G D Valentine* 42
Mountain Vigil *Douglas Fraser* 42
The Wilderness *Kathleen Raine* 43
Hills *Robin Munro* 44

THE LENGTH OF THE LAND

At Kirk Yetholm *David Calder* 47
In the Cheviots *Maurice Lindsay* 47
St Mary's Loch *Geoffrey Faber* 48
Shadows Among the Ettrick Hills *William Addison* 48
On Ellson Fell *William Landles* 49
Grey Galloway *Thomas S Cairncross* 49
Apprentices *Robin Munro* 50
Remembered Melody *Andrew Lang* 50
A Border Burn *J B Selkirk* 51
If I Were Old *Will H Ogilvie* 52
A Border Forecast *William Landles* 52
Leap in the Smoke *John Buchan* 53
The Ochil Hills *Anon* 54
The Twinkling Earn *John Davidson* 54
The Gean Trees *Violet Jacob* 55
Ane to Anither *Duncan Glen* 56

Inversnaid *Gerard Manley Hopkins* 58
There is Snowdrift on the Mountain *W P Ker* 58
Winter Climb *Beinn Eunaich* 59
Snow Crystals on Meall Glas *Elizabeth A Wilson* 60
Under Creag Mhor *Stewart Conn* 61
For Summer's Here *Ratcliffe Barnett* 62
One of the Many Days *Norman MacCaig* 62
On Ben Dorain *Duncan Ban Macintyre* 63
Deer at the Roadside *Iain Crichton Smith* 64
Envoy *Alasdair Maclean* 65
Passin Ben Dorain *Alastair Mackie* 66
Rannoch Moor *Malcolm MacGregor* 67
Rannoch, by Glencoe *T S Eliot* 67
Buachaille Etive Mor and Buachaille Etive Beag *Naomi Mitchison* 68
Glencoe *G K Chesterton* 68
The Lost Valley *Gordon J Gadsby* 69
Bidean Nam Bian *A M Dobson* 70
On the Croun o Bidean *J K Annand* 72
Corries *Janet M Smith* 73
Schiehallion *Helen Cruickshank* 74
Hauf-roads up Schiehallion *Donald Campbell* 76
Loch Ossian *Syd Scroggie* 77
Ben Alder 1963-1977 *Des Hannigan* 77
Night Expedition from Ben Alder Cottage *Roger A Redfern* 78
Space and Time *Syd Scroggie* 79
Staoineag *Leen Volwerk* 79
The Harlot *Hamish Brown* 80
Hut *G J F Dutton* 81
Eagle *Tom Bowker* 82
Written Upon the Top of Ben Nevis *John Keats* 82
Climbing Zero Gully *David J Morley* 83
Drumochter *Anne B Murray* 84
The Boar of Badenoch and the Sow of Atholl *Naomi Mitchison* 84
The Road *Christine Orr* 85
Beinn A'Ghlo *Bill Tulloch* 86
Lochan *Roger Smith* 86
Long Ago *Syd Scroggie* 87
Caenlochan *Helen B Cruickshank* 88
Change and Immutability *Syd Scroggie* 88
Foxgloves and Snow *Marion Angus* 89
The Patriot *J C Milne* 89
Bennachie *Charles Murray* 90
In Lythe Strathdon *Charles Murray* 91
The Drunken Dee *Syd Scroggie* 91
In Praise of Ben Avon *Brenda G Macrow* 92
Benighted to the Foothills of the Cairngorms *Olive Fraser* 93
At the Shelter-stone *Brenda G Macrow* 94
Dolomites *J C Milne* 95

The Silent Walls *Ian Strachan* 95
Highland Shooting Lodge *Maurice Lindsay* 96
The Hill Burns *Nan Shepherd* 96
Wind *Hamish Brown* 98
The Lairig *J C Milne* 98
Sgoran Dhu *Nan Shepherd* 98
Cairngorm, November 1971 *Martyn Berry* 99
Beyond Feith Buidhe *Hamish Brown* 100
Rothiemurchus *Colin Lamont* 100
The Spirit of the Cairngorms *Axel Firsoff* 101
Aviemore *Janet Waller* 102
Stopping by Shadows *Robin Fulton* 102
Far in the West *Douglas Fraser* 103
Theme and Variations *W P Ker* 104
Nettles *Neil Munro* 104
The Shieling *Edward Thomas* 105
Glen Rosa *William Jeffrey* 106
A Picture *D C Cuthbertson* 107
The Paps of Jura *Andrew Young* 107
Island of Mull *Dugald Macphail* 108
There are Gods *G L Riley* 108
The Island of Rhum *Roy Ferguson* 109
Nightmare on Rhum *James Macmillan* 110
The Ancient Speech *Kathleen Raine* 111
Glen Pean *Denis Rixson* 112
Hill Love *James Macmillan* 112
The Road Moves On *Dorothy Nash* 113
Leac A'Chlarsair *Lucy Taylor* 114
The Coolin Ridge *William Bell* 114
The Witch *Wilfrid Gibson* 115
Skye *John Gawsworth* 115
Beckon Me, Ye Cuillins *K G P Hendrie* 116
Skye Summer *Islay Murray Donaldson* 117
Kinloch Ainort *Sorley MacLean* 117
No Voice of Man *Raymond Falconer* 118
Sgurr Nan Gillean *Sorley MacLean* 119
Ye Simple Men *John Stuart Blackie* 120
A Warning *Alexander Nicholson* 120
Doing the Dubhs *Anon* 121
Coruisk *W C Smith* 121
A'Chuilionn *A G Hutchinson* 122
From Skye, Early Autumn *M L Michal* 122
The Misty Island *Anon* 122
Soaring *Cal Clothier* 123
View *Robin Munro* 124
Oreads *Kathleen Raine* 125
The Dam, Glen Garry *Robert Symmons* 126
April, Glengarry *Philip Coxon* 126

The Falls of Glomach *Andrew Young* 127
Wester Ross *Naomi Mitchison* 127
The Things of the North *Rennie McOwan* 128
Climb in Torridon (Liathach, 1947) *Brenda G Macrow* 128
Loch Luichart *Andrew Young* 129
What Finer Hills? *J K Annand* 130
Dundonnel Mountains *Andrew Young* 130
Highland Region *Victor Price* 131
Above Inverkirkaig *Norman MacCaig* 132
Moment Musical in Assynt *Norman MacCaig* 133
Ascent *Donald G Saunders* 133
High Up on Suilven *Norman MacCaig* 134
No Accident *Norman MacCaig* 134
Assynt *Alan Gilchrist* 135
What Are You Thinking About? *James Macmillan* 135
Prospect of a Mountain *Andrew Young* 136
On Foinaven *Donald G Saunders* 136
Marry the Lass? *Andrew Greig* 137
Marriage on a Mountain Ridge *Stewart Conn* 138
The Strath of Kildonan *Betty Morris* 140
At a Ruined Croft *John Manson* 140
The Tall Sky *Arthur Ball* 141
More Than People *Robin Fulton* 141
Above Ben Loyal *Arthur Ball* 142
Lion Gate *Vera Rich* 142
Roads *George Mackay Brown* 143
Shetland, Hill Dawn *Robin Munro* 144
Ronas Hill *Hamish Brown* 144

A CERTAIN FRIVOLITY

The Lost Leader *Douglas Fraser* 147
The Old Munro Bagger *Anon* 148
Mountain Days *Barclay Fraser* 149
The Last of the Grand Old Masters *Tom Patey* 150
Macinnes's Mountain Patrol *Tom Patey* 152
Weather Rhymes *Hamish Brown* 153
To a Midge *Eilidh Nisbet* 154 ✓
Motive for Mercy *Ken Milburn* 155
Aye, There's Hills *Hamish Brown* 155
The Scottish Mountaineering Club Song *John G Stott* 156
The Battle of Glentilt (1847) *Sir Douglas Maclagan* 158
Southward Bound *J F A Burt* 161
Feels *J C Milne* 161
Sisyphus *Robert Garioch* 162
Canedolia *Edwin Morgan* 163

A BACKWARD VIEW FROM THE CAIRN

Levavi Oculos *Marion Campbell*	167
On the Heights *W K Holmes*	168
Mountaineering Bus *Rennie McOwan*	169
How Small is Man *John Stuart Blackie*	170
What Called Me to the Heights? *Lawrence Pilkington*	170
The Old Mountaineer *W K Holmes*	171
The Perfect Garden *Winifred Robertson*	172
On the Hill *William Soutar*	172
To Alan *Douglas Fraser*	173
Then and Now *Anne B Murray*	174
Footprints *Hamish Brown*	175
Among High Hills *William Soutar*	175
A Wind from the West *Lachlan MacLean Watt*	176
Ante Mortem *Syd Scroggie*	177
Growing Old *Douglas Fraser*	178
The Hillman Looks Back *Rennie McOwan*	179
When I Am Dead *Hugh Barrie*	180
When I Die *Brenda G Macrow*	181
One Thousand Feet of Shadow *David Craig*	181
Looking Down a Hill *A R Thompson*	182
Mountain Greed *Hugh C Rae*	183
Faur Wid I Dee? *J C Milne*	184
To This Hill Again *James Macmillan*	184
The Hills of God *A A Buist*	185
Poem, 1972 *Syd Scroggie*	186
At Last *Syd Scroggie*	188
Blows the Wind Today *Robert Louis Stevenson*	188
ACKNOWLEDGEMENTS AND INDEX OF AUTHORS	189
INDEX OF FIRST LINES	197

Introduction

When Martyn Berry and I eventually met we discovered we had both, for many years, been copying down poems about the British hills. We soon decided to combine forces and prepare an anthology of twentieth century British and Irish mountain verse. There has never been a comprehensive anthology and the response to the idea was encouraging.

We soon found that the material accumulating was particularily rich on Scottish mountains so, while still welcoming material for the British volume, we decided I should go ahead with a purely Scottish anthology. This would give us time to find material for some 'gaps' in the more general volume. In the Scottish one we could also permit dialect poems and slip back to older work as well. Sadly, Gaelic poetry is only briefly touched on in translation. The hills form such a background to the Highland culture that few poems actually are fully hill pieces, however much permeated by the atmosphere. Recreational mountain activities are comparatively recent phenomenon after all, and the majority of the poems in this collection reflect this modern surge of interest.

This collection would not have been possible without the help of scores of people. They are thanked (see p 189) and I hope the list of poets will encourage further reading. I am most grateful to Norman MacCaig for agreeing to write the Foreword.

In the end this is a personal choice but I have tried to select for wide-ranging reasons. If some spark brightens a poem I have not hesitated to include it, regardless of style, ideas, or even literary merit. (Not everyone can lead a Very Severe climb.) Space has excluded some longer poems and some have been held back for the British anthology. This is a collection for the hill-goer's pack rather than a literary or historical study for some aesthetic Mountain Leadership Certificate. Come to it as we do to the hill, with rambling opportunism. Here is a guide book, but you must make the climb.

HAMISH BROWN

21 Carlin Craig
Kinghorn

For
Martyn Berry
and all those who helped
put feet to this dream

Questions and Answers

SCOTLAND SMALL?

Scotland small? Our multiform, our infinite Scotland *small?*
Only as a patch of hillside may be a cliché corner
To a fool who cries 'Nothing but heather!' Where in September
  another
Sitting there and resting and gazing round
Sees not only heather but blaeberries
With bright green leaves and leaves already turned scarlet,
Hiding ripe blue berries; and amongst the sage-green leaves
Of the bog-myrtle the golden flowers of the tormentil shining;
And on the small bare places, where the little Blackface sheep
Found grazing, milkworts blue as summer skies;
And down in neglected peat-hags, not worked
In living memory, sphagnum moss in pastel shades
Of yellow, green, and pink; sundew and butterwort
And nodding harebells vying in their colour
With the blue butterflies that poise themselves delicately upon
  them.
And stunted rowans with harsh dry leaves of glorious colour
'Nothing but heather!'—How marvellously descriptive! And
  incomplete!

HUGH MACDIARMID

IN THE HIGHLANDS

In the highlands, in the country places,
Where the old plain men have rosy faces,
And the young fair maidens
    Quiet eyes;
Where essential silence cheers and blesses,
And for ever in the hill-recesses
Her more lovely music
    Broods and dies.

O to mount again where erst I haunted;
Where the old red hills are bird-enchanted,
And the low green meadows
    Bright with sward;
And when even dies, the million-tinted,
And the night has come, and planets glinted,
    Lamp-bestarred.

O to dream, O to awake and wander
There, and with delight to take and render,
Through the trance of silence,
    Quiet breath;
Lo! for there, among the flowers and grasses,
Only the mightier movement sounds and
      passes;
Only winds and rivers,
    Life and death.

ROBERT LOUIS STEVENSON

OLDER NOW

Older now,
with grey where once was brown,
I came back to you, my memory land.
You did not let me down.
Once more amongst the clean skies,
the mountains and the streams,
I found again that peace of mind,
that quiet to soothe my dreams.
I felt the years roll back,
could feel both wild and free
amongst the solitude of hills
that kept their faith with me.

DAVE GINGELL

LAST JOURNEY
(from *The Testament of John Davidson*)

Oh, long before the bere was steeped for malt,
  And long before the grape was crushed for wine,
The glory of the march without a halt,
  The triumph of a stride like yours and mine
Was known to folk like us, who walked about,
To be the sprightliest cordial out and out!
    Folk like us, with hearts that beat,
      Sang it too in sun and rain—
      'Heel and toe from dawn to dusk,
      Round the world and home again.'

My feet are heavy now, but on I go,
　My head erect beneath the tragic years.
The way is steep, but I would have it so;
　And dusty, but I lay the dust with tears,
Though none can see me weep: alone I climb
The rugged path that leads me out of time—
　　　Out of time and out of all,
　　　　Singing yet in sun and rain,
　　　　'Heel and toe from dawn to dusk,
　　　　Round the world and home again.'

JOHN DAVIDSON

THE PEAK

We sailed in sunshine; but the glen was black
As Tartarus with raven clouds that swirled
In a fantastic frenzy, closely furled
One moment round the hills; now, streaming, torn
To ribbons; then in bundling fleeces whirled
As in a witch's cauldron, leaving bare
The jagged ranges to the pallid glare
Of lightning: and we heard the thunder crack
In short sharp volleys like quick rifle-fire:
Then once again the firth in instant night
Was blotted out; while still in lively light
We sailed serenely on through the blue morn
Towards the islands of our heart's desire.

But, ere we lost the land, a brooding cloud
On the horizon, suddenly the shroud
Slipped from the shoulders of a single peak
That soared in sunshine like a soul set free
Of the gross turmoil of mortality:
And, as we gazed, our hearts, too full to speak,
Found in that vision all we sailed to seek.

WILFRID GIBSON

HIGHLAND LOVES

Can one love a boulder
gritted and grey
and in the normal way
perched on the shoulder
of some obscure hill,
with heather shoots,
tiny and still,
peeping out from
crevice and crack and
adding soft colour to
unchanging rock?

Can one love the rain
marching in lances
across the tops
until light changes and
the swishing drops
alter the stones,
and amid dull hues yellow
lichen flashes and green
moss and amber tones
of different veins are
freshly embossed?

Can one love the birds,
brown, quick and small
with their darting flight
and piping calls
until by some trait of
movement or mark
they become known
like friends and
thus identified help
to captivate our
moorland hearts?

Can one love a tree
like this solitary birch,
judged as 'a weed'
and thereby besmirched

by those who do not know
its blinding beauty
against dwindling snow
and are unaware that it
cannot be 'classified'
but is love itself
realised.

RENNIE McCOWAN

ROCK, BE MY DREAM

Rock, be my dream—
Immense stillness of rock curved under the land.
Dark stone ripened on the sun-core of the world
Be the sphere of my peace.
The flame that fore-ran your deep strength
Has fathered my blood, and built wholeness within me.
Under the loam of my thoughts, broken with passing harvests,
Rock, be my dream, a burning fulfilled.

MacKNIGHT BLACK

FREEDOM OF THE HILLS

Mine is the freedom of the tranquil hills
When vagrant breezes bend the sinewy grass,
While sunshine on the widespread landscape spills
And light as down the fleet cloud-shadows pass.

Mine, still, that freedom when the storm clouds race,
Cracking their whips against defiant crags
And mists swirl boiling up from inky space
To vanish on the instant, torn to rags.

When winter grips the mountains in a vice,
Silently stifling with its pall of snow,
Checking the streams, clasping the rocks in ice,
Still to the mantled summits I would go.

Sun-drenched, I sense the message they impart,
Storm-lashed, I hear it sing through every vein;
Among the snows it whispers to my heart
'Here is your freedom. Taste—and come again!'

DOUGLAS FRASER

OWRE THE HILL

Wha gangs wi' us owre the hill
And is baith far and near?
Abüne the bluid that lifts and fa's
Anither hert we hear.

Wha gangs wi' us owre the hill,
On earth and in the sky,
And is as hainless to our hands
As the wild bird's cry?

WILLIAM SOUTAR

THE SPELL O' THE HILLS

I'm growin auld, I'm growin cauld,
My bluid rins sluggish noo;
Nae mair my hert is like to stert
The flush upon my broo.
And, fegs, it's lang sin' lass or sang
Has gart me catch my breith,
But still ae spell, it's trith to tell,
Will last until my deith.

Its' the auld spell, the young spell,
The spell the Hielands cast;
The lang spell, the strang spell,
That aye for me will last;
The clear spell, the dear spell
I canna lang resist
O' the fair hills, the bare hills
In sun, snaw or mist.

I've settled doun upon the toun;
I warsle on wi' thrift
At mean pursuits, while reek pollutes
The grey, unhailsome lift.
But whiles I see afore my ee
A vision o' the glens:
It's then I lang to rise and gang
Amang the michty bens.

Oh the green hills, the clean hills,
I lue them weel aneuch,
But mair still the bare hills
Wi' mony a craig and cleugh;
The rouch hills, the teugh hills
That froun dour and grim,
The hie hills, the stey hills,
They daur ye to sclim.

It's weel I ken in yonder glen
The birks are gleamin bricht;
The burn lowps doun sae brisk and broun
And sparkles in the licht.
The braes ablow wi' heather glow,
The peak that soars abune
Will find, I hope, upon its slope
My dodderin fitsteps sune.

For the auld spell, the young spell,
Is coost on me again;
The lang spell, the strang spell
That has me aye to hain.
The fair hills, the bare hills,
The hills wild and free,
Will ca' me and draw me
Until the day I dee.

DOUGLAS FRASER

AND HAPPY AM I

The soot on the cassies,
The drunk on the seat,
The jute on the lassies,
The fog in the street;
The gleam in the shutter,
The smell of the fry,
The fag in the gutter,
 Unhappy am I.

The moss on the boulder,
The sun in the glen,
The cloud on the shoulder,
The snow on the ben;
The deer on the rigging,
The lark in the sky,
A friend in the bigging,
 And happy am I.

SYD SCROGGIE

WINE O LIVING

Hae ye smelt the tang o heather
  And the rich pitch pine,
    Or the bracken birstled yellow wi the sun?
O the moon abune the lochan
  Hae ye seen the siller shine,
    Looming eerie through the drift upon the dun?

Hae ye traiked it up Glen Ogle
  By your lane, sane sel?
    Hae ye crossed the Moor o Rannoch in the mist?
Were ye boggit to the buttocks?
  Did ye hear the eagles yell?
    Were ye frichted by the adders when they hissed?

Hae ye whupped the whurling eddies
  By the brow'd, loud linn?
    Hae ye tracked the tired buck upon the brae?
When ye couched it in the heather
  Were ye chittered by the win?
    Hae ye waukened in the mist at skreigh o day?

And the Islands, hae ye seen em
  In the wet, wet West,
    Wi the kelp a-clinging crisp abune the tide?
Hae ye heard the girning gullies?
  Seen the singing seals at rest?
    Hae ye raced the ocean stallions when they ride?

Gin ye kenna what's ma meaning,
  Gin ye think ma havers daft,
    Ach, I'd liefer blaw ma breath upon the breeze!
Ye've no quaffed the quaich o Living
  In a steep, deep draught—
    Never lipped the wine o Living to the lees!

                                        MATT MARSHALL

THE KINGSHIP OF THE HILLS

Born in the purple the red grouse cry;
Born in the purple the whaups reply;
Born in the purple the clouds are kings
Sailing away on their snow-white wings.
The eagle high on the ruby peak
Has the scorn o' the vale in his curling beak;
And every burn that goes dancing down
Has a purple robe and a silver crown.

The lightnings flash like a jewel-band;
The thunder rolls like a king's command;
With a palace-roof of the windy stars
Where God looks over His golden bars.
Here, in the pride of all high-born things
The red deer go with the gait of kings;
And only a step from their cottage doors
The rough hill-shepherds are emperors.

W. H. OGILVIE

AT EUSTON

Stranger with the pile of luggage proudly labelled
   for Portree,
How I wish, this night of August, I were you and
   you were me!
Think of all that lies before you when the train
   goes sliding forth
And the lines athwart the sunset lead you swiftly
   to the North!
Think of breakfast at Kingussie, think of high
   Drumochter Pass,
Think of Highland breezes singing through the
   bracken and the grass,
Scabious blue and yellow daisy, tender fern beside
   the train,
Rowdy Tummel falling, brawling, seen and lost
   and glimpsed again!
You will pass my golden roadway of the days of
   long ago;
Will you realise the magic of the names I used to
   know:

Clachnaharry, Achnashellach, Achnasheen, and
    Duirinish?
Ev'ry moor alive with coveys, ev'ry pool aboil
    with fish?
Ev'ry well-remembered vista more exciting mile by
    mile
Till the wheeling gulls are screaming round the
    engine at the Kyle.
Think of cloud on Bheinn na Cailleach, jagged
    Cuchullins soaring high,
Scent of peat and all the glamour of the misty Isle of
    Skye!

A. M. HARBORD

I LEAVE TONIGHT FROM EUSTON

I shall leave tonight from Euston
By the seven-thirty train,
And from Perth in the early morning
I shall see the hills again.
From the top of Ben Macdhui
I shall watch the gathering storm,
And see the crisp snow lying
At the back of Cairngorm.
I shall feel the mist from Bhrotain
And pass by Lairig Ghru
To look on dark Loch Einich
From the heights of Sgoran Dubh.
From the broken Barns of Bynack
I shall see the sunrise gleam
On the forehead of Ben Rinnes
And Strathspey awake from dream.
And again in the dusk of evening
I shall find once more alone
The dark water of the Green Loch,
And the pass beyond Ryvoan.
For tonight I leave from Euston
And leave the world behind;
Who has the hills as a lover,
Will find them wondrous kind.

ANON

Written on the door of Ryvoan Bothy and fortunately copied before lost

FOR TONY, DOUGAL, MICK, BUGS, NICK *ET AL*

How can we justify a life,
spent sitting by the coal?
or roaring at the stadium,
foul ref; off side, goal?

And how do we justify the time,
spent staring at the set?
or in the boozer sinking pints,
or placing one more bet?

And tell us how we justify,
the attitude today?
that even if we shirk the work,
we still expect the pay?

How can we justify a life,
without a plan or vision?
with never a constructive thought,
no risks and no ambition?

And yet we sit and criticise,
the spirit wild and free,
who climbs the highest mountain,
or sails the cruelest sea,
who plumbs the deepest ocean,
or explores the darkest cave,
or has the crazy notion,
to surf the biggest wave.

Blinded by security,
we say they must be fools,
to shoot white water rapids,
or fight fast whirlpool;
but a true appreciation,
of life we'll never know,
till we've pushed our minds and bodies,
as far as they can go,
and if death should overtake us,
then death must have been due,
but there is no sting in death,
no sting for you.

DAVE BATHGATE

13

OF ONLY A SINGLE POEM

above the plains
mountains flourish,
white, distracting eyes
at intersections.

they are cold, frequently
dangerous, always
exhausting and when you come down
are still there.

then why climb them?
say your constituents
say the headbellies say
the paunchbrains not knowing

what it is to represent them
what it is to be the guest
dirty unapologetic
of even a minor pinnacle.

G. J. F. DUTTON

O AA THE MANLY SPORTS

Lowpin owre a burn,
Slunkin throu a moss,
Is better nor the corner and
A game at pitch and toss.

Scruntin on a boulder,
Scartin on a slab,
Wi wind and sun upon your face
Is juist the very dab.

Warslin up a chimley,
Speelin up a craig,
Sure-fitted as a mountain gait
Or noble royal staig.

Poised upon a traiverse
On a mountain waa
Taks the stuff to mak the man
That dings doun aa.

Breengin throu a snaw-wreath,
Smoolin up on ice,
A fig for creeshie fireside folk
That think we arena wyce!

Pechin up a brae
Or skytin doun a scree,
For wale o aa the manly sports
Climbin bears the gree.

J. K. ANNAND

THREE GIRLS ON A BUTTRESS

You've got halfway, and found it rather hard.
Well, harder than you'd thought.
You sweated somewhat freely as you fought
Unrhythmically upward.
The rope snaked out beneath you as you climbed:
Too much snake-rope, crawling along behind
While you traced awkwardly your slimy track—
And now it's obvious you can't get back.

O Woman! How inelegant you are!
Feet, knees and elbows clumsy in the crack.
You're stuck! Oh, Goodness. Now you're looking back
At two white upturned faces watching you.
They think you can get up!
O Woman! How incongruous you are!

. . . Oh Joy! A whopping spike
Just six feet up. A few more heaves . . .
We're there . . . pop on a runner . . . Ah!
Relax and breathe, clinging . . .

Now on again.
Two hazy faces will you to go up
This greasy unrelenting crack,
And so you do (the snake
Of rope still writhing up behind)
To claw at last
A shelf of grass
With careful standing room enough
For three.

A thread belay, and up the others come,
Clawing and flailing too.
(O Woman! How ridiculous you are!)

The next pitch is another much the same ...

... But suddenly the angle falls away,
And rapidly
You romp aloft, and finish it
Rather the worse for wear,
But too content at heart
To care.

EILIDH NISBET

PITCH SEVEN

It is consummation, a mad rape
Of earth's solid resisting; mute
Limbs thrusting, hands grasping,
Minds godworn, craving a primitive substitute.

It is not
Behaviour as was always there!
Outworn creeds, too simple
For our fractured, shackled, nightmare understanding.
We were content once, or dreamt we were,
Before the plastic age
Before the bomb
Before free love
Free milk
Free doom.

Agag no longer tip-toes,
Tripping with a virgin wonder.
Jericho's walls are broken down
For glory, death and plunder.

It is substitution, a dagger desperation
Ripping bare the nakedness of men.
Why?

Because we must
Engage the body to liberate the mind,
Embrace earth rock to find a soul.

It is all the deep things of long ago
Swept away, then phoenix born
For a new generation.
We may not understand, God knows,
But still we climb.

Take in the tangled slack!

HAMISH BROWN

ROCK LEADER

Fingers aching, nails breaking,
legs quaking, foot shaking,
tired, tortured toes.

Rope dragging, second nagging,
muscles flagging, slings snagging,
upward still he goes.

Windblowing, pace slowing,
light going, just knowing,
not a place to pose.

Can't make it, chance, take it,
hold? fake it, mind wake it,
fear and doubt enclose.

Slimy wet groove, made the last move,
what does it prove? only that you've,
climbed it, I suppose.

―――――――

Old climbers never die, they just run out of rope.

DAVE BATHGATE

17

THE CLIMBER SURVEYS HIS MOUNTAIN

Here I stand
Mouthing the air like a salmon,
My eye hooked to the gully's line,
The consequence
My faith will follow.

From the rock
I choose without words the only line
And will make what I see now,
Creating sweat and balance there
From this idea.

When I climb,
Three pressure points, precise, pure,
To the expected summit—
No confusion, no wrong choices,
But the view,
Reward and release,
Of Rannoch, Schiehallion and Mamore.

HUGH OUSTON

MAGMA

Climbers are fools, forget
What burns below,
Pluto's King—
What price their ice and snow,

Their high so tricky prize
On one day's granite?
Night unties
It all to bloody blankets

Or a bird in the bag.
Deliberately
They borrowed a crag
And plotted against the heart's

Tumult: they crystallised
Their brief desire
Impossibly close
To the rich destroying fire.

G. J. F. DUTTON

18

ON FALLING
(from *Men on Ice*)

No,
people are feared to fall *off*
and *out*

off the ledge
off the boil
out of sight
out of their minds

You be sure and fall *in*
and you'll take deep rest
in your depression
when you fall as we all
do right down some terrible night
the spirit of gravity
locked round your shoulders
down through all the levels
into the ragged hole
in the heart
of the heart,

then
when you can fall no further
when everything is permitted
but nothing is worth it

walls fall away
mountains are as glass
wind plays violins
on the other side of the ice

Then the eye recoils from nothing
and you never know fear again

You call mountaineers insane?
Their eyes are calm
surviving smoothly
in a monstrous environment . . .

ANDREW GREIG

THE CLIMBING ROPE

When one climber fell to his doom, I also fell,
Stunned by the stone that smashed his living grace,
And rent my life asunder. An abyss
Of stony grief received me. There I lay
In the dank dark, uncaring as the dead,
Scarce moving, numb and lifeless with my loss.

The sound I heard was substance: the fugal strands
Seemed a rope cable, stalwart and secure,
Let down from Heaven into my pit of Hell,
Woven by human hands: the great-souled Bach
Twined the stout cords for succour of such as I.
Paid out by human hands too: on the keys
The fingers moved, plaiting and replicating
The murmurous design, at once simple and subtle
As those interwoven borders wherein the Celt
With endless fluid line, portrayed eternity.

I raised my head: there was blue sky above
The chill blank walls that hemmed me in. To the touch
The rope was reassuring, firm, secure,
Belayed by the old musician's faith to some
Pinnacle on the heavenly skyline. They
Were living hands that paid it out through the keys
Of the clear-toned instrument aptly to my need.
Here in this pit of death no need to cower
While the soft persuasive voices so discoursed
Of love, joy, flawless peace.

> And over and over
>   Its strands interweaving
> In a pattern of true
>   And of trustful believing
> The music led upwards,
> Twined, twisted, climbed upwards,
> Strong succour, the saving
>   Support of my soul.

So I won free: not soon, nor suddenly
Does one lift one's head clear of the gulf of grief
Into warm sunlight and the honest day.
Hard the slow climb from a chasm so profound.
But the climbing rope let down to me by God's
Good grace, that steadied me on the long ascent
Was woven (blessèd be his name) by Bach.

A. V. STUART

IN MEMORIAM

This is not the way to die—
a broken body on the scree
battered by a fall of several hundred feet.
We came through the night to save,
not to sit and shiver
a few feet from your grave,
exchanging words to pass the hours of night.

When dawn comes we will go
with you to the valley once again.
Your blood still stains the snow,
but now you know no pain—
now the night has gone and it is dawn.

You died before we came,
broken by these hills which have no love nor hate of men.
You were just a name,
a man who died, as men will die again,
as long as there are hills, or seas, or unknown parts
to stir the wandering urges in searching human hearts.

DAVE GINGELL

ON A LEDGE

On a ledge of rock he lay;
facing north he lay to stare
through the crystal sea of air.
For, lit by the declining day,
the mountains waited, range on range,
(who could tell how far away?)—
more than he might recognise.
There were many that were strange,
and many that he seemed to know:
there the scattered Grampians,
from the Cairngorms to Glencoe,
kept no secret from his eyes:
even as the future lies
in the mind of him who plans
a holiday—so many weeks'
delight in merely being young
under the Coolin mist, among
the solitudes, and on the peaks.

Yet even there is discontent:
only the mountains are at peace,
the summit snows themselves resent
all winter their imprisonment.
Celebrating their release
in Spring the foaming waters pour
down the corries to the lochs
where every wave that laps the shore
and slaps against the rounded rocks
implores a man to strip and swim,
(since all the colour of the lake
needs the whiteness of a limb,
as a ridge of snow can make
the blue of heaven more intense.)
Even there he would desire
the distant ridge, would sigh for those
ranges further to the north,
colder, sharper, more immense;
every morning setting forth
to reach a higher waste of snows.
And far away the future grew
faint as the very distant past,
for rank on rank the mountains rose
toward the horizon, where at last
the same untroubled flood of blue
covered those shining domes of snow
and the unconquered crests of cloud.
Then gratefully he rose to go.
And his companion sitting bowed
over him, watching his gentle breath
stir the foam of blood upon
his lips, knew first that he was gone
by no accustomed mark of death,
but the range of nose and brow
shadowed by the slanting sun
suddenly appeared to grow
more remote, more sharp and colder
than the mountains of the moon,
and he remembered, even so,
in the Alps one afternoon
looking back across his shoulder,
he saw the peak which he had trod
with the Angelus was grown
innocent, and stood alone

WILLIAM BELL

NN 616410

There's no track
back through
the boulders
and heather, only
deer roads
wander and
idiot sheep trails
cling to
a bare living.

The hillside unwinds
into
an abyss.
Cloud fronds
swirl by.
The unbelievable
compass
knows its way
steep down through
a scatter of rocks
above the col.

The next mass
rises ahead
into and out of
blind cloud.

High wind
tears at the cairn.
Held up on
the crown of the mountain
we offer ourselves
to the enshrouding
emptiness.

                    BILL TULLOCH

ONE WAY DOWN

The scree empties down the mountain,
The stone under me constantly changes,
A stance of a sort, making it possible
Neither to stop nor fall headlong.
Amongst the glacial rubbish I can reach out,
Pick myself a piece, and make something of it:
A face of grey crystals, a good stone to hold,
An egg-shaped bird-body, the likeness of a skull.
It is hard to keep even the best ones
Or hand them over to secure bystanders
Watching from the edge of this paralysed torrent.
At a steep place I turn a somersault,
Land with a crunch, resume the long crumbling.
The floor of the corrie turns from a map
To a pelt of deer's-hair sedge and blaeberry
And stunted rowans rooting into the peat.
Now the rock-face rises to the full,
Rears over with an evening darkness.
The pools lie flat and shallow and black
As death, the ultimate absence of qualities.

DAVID CRAIG

ON WALKING BACK TO THE BUS

The sun was sinking when we reached the glen,
And rouged the snow-clad peaks on either hand.
Tired limbs had chastened self's too shrill demand,
And freed our souls to roam beyond its ken.
Silent, we tramped the fallen leaves. But when
We halted as we crossed the burn, and scanned
The scene, dark waters surged o'er rock and sand,
Yet mirrored clear the bright and distant Ben.

Is it for this we toil up many a hill,
To glimpse at beauty with unclouded eye?
Or is it but to exercise our will,
To scale a thousand tops before we die?
You'll say, no doubt, 'tis both of these; and still
Give other reasons, too. And yet ask why?

ALAN GARDNER

ON LOOKING AT AN OLD CLIMBING PHOTOGRAPH

I have been there
High on that rock perch. Beneath my feet
A thousand feet of air
And far below the moor spread like a map,
The mountains crowding round
Waiting to hear the roll-call of their names:
Some, valued friends recalling splendid climbs,
Some still to meet, sending their challenge out
For future days.

We felt like giants, sitting there at ease
With half of Scotland in our view,
Though hours before
We seemed insignificant as ants
As we peered upwards at those mighty crags.
Yet slowly we advanced,
Muscles responding as the need arose
Effort and craft achieved their goal at last
And that reward
Which climbers know but cannot well explain.
What need—so long as they can climb again?

DOUGLAS FRASER

HILLS OF THE MIDDLE DISTANCE

Hills of the middle distance: crooked backs,
    heavy with winter snow;
Trails of the nearer foreground: frozen tracks,
    leading us where to go.
Journeys in ice-bound landscapes: shade and light,
    perspectives that reveal
Worlds of new dimensions: depth and height,
    pain and the power to heal.
Healing for so much sorrow: mountain balm,
    backcloth of happiness;
Hills of the middle distance: storm and calm,
    each with its friendliness.

ARCHIE MITCHELL

A SONG OF DEGREES

Half a mile from the shining sea
  The roses hang, at the edge of the wood,
Under the oak and the hazel tree,
  And there to rest is good.

Half way up from the rosy place,
  Within the foldings of the hill,
There you may find the desolate face
  Of upland waters still.

Half way over the towering land,
  The mountains glisten, the winds go by,
Where rocks of adamant understand
  The secrets of the sky.

W. P. KER

THE QUIET GLEN

Larks trill in the quiet glen,
The burn skips on the boulders.
Winds ruffle the smooth ben
Where sheep browse on its shoulders.

Here have been only nights and days,
Sun and the clouds sailing,
Moon and stars that went their ways
And the dusk's soft veiling.

Nothing has changed since time began
But the slow ebb of the seasons.
Go your ways, you questing man;
Life has no need of reasons.

DOUGLAS FRASER

SILVER IN THE WIND

The ptarmigan cries across the corrie,
sounds fading again in the grip of icy wind
that races fast on cliff wall and lichened gully;
beloved mountain, the wind blows silver,
there is silver in the wind.

A solitary hind, watchful, scans the ridge,
then, in silence, becomes invisible, stealing away from sight
to appear again, silhouetted on the crest, then to vanish;
mist on the mountain, the wind blows silver,
there is silver in the wind.

Where the timid adder sleeps, a fox moves, gliding,
skirting scree, above the loch, the surface still and frozen,
the air fills, as flakes carry from pinnacle to corrie wall;
mountain of snow, the wind blows silver,
there is silver in the wind.

Soon the peak lies below a white mantle,
snow cornices lining ragged rims, the climber turns away,
descending to seek protection in sheltered rocks;
mountain of storms, the wind blows silver,
there is silver in the wind.

IAN STRACHAN

THE DIPPER

Here where the river is slender and small,
Tumbling like a child over stones in its fall
From pool to pool,
Here where the slant willow leans her breast
Over the secret of a dipper's nest,
The dipper himself stands all alone
Bowing to the river from his platform of stone.
How dapperly in black he bows with his back
To the strings in the stream,
And the sunlight-fingered harp
Touched into music on the sharp-edged stones,
To the bright trombones,
And the horns and the flutes,
And the reedy clarinets whose woodland undertones
Murmur in the river from the alders at the edge,
From the rustle in the sedge.

27

How assuredly in white he bows from left to right
To the river that he faces with endearing, sprightly graces.
The emerald-handed crowfoot is bearing cups of white;
And tiny-tendoned cresses are caught in weeds' caresses
In river-traps of light.
And from his rocky rostrum the dipper bows, and blesses
Every river sound and sight.

PHOEBE HESKETH

THE HOODED CROW

Perched on a birch stump
the hoodie sits, beady
eyes swivelling, head a-twitch.
A dirk for a beak and a
croak for a song. It's
death for the weak and
life for the strong.

Grey-coated murderer, and
killer of fawns, eater of
offal and terror of lambs.
A lover of cruelty and
gouger of eyes, your
scavenging flights end
in pitiful cries.

There's no good word
for you, harsh bird of the
north, save one, save one,
the place of your birth.
Like a sentinel marking
the northern bounds, you
tell of a change, dramatic,
profound.

To see you means wildness
and mountains and glens,
and the hills of the Highlands
around us again. You're a
cold-blooded slayer of the
frail and the weak. Why are
you part of the world that
we seek?

RENNIE McCOWAN

THE ECHOING CLIFF

White gulls that sit and float
Each on his shadow like a boat,
Sandpipers, oystercatchers
And herons, those grey stilted watchers,
From loch and corran rise,
And as they scream and squawk abuse
Echo from wooded cliff replies
So clearly that the dark pine boughs,
Where goldcrests flit
And owls in drowsy wisdom sit,
Are filled with sea-birds and their cries.

ANDREW YOUNG

EAGLES AND ISLES

Eagles and isles and uncompanioned peaks,
The self-reliant isolated things
Release my soul, embrangled in the stress
Of all day's crass and cluttered business:
Release my soul in song, and give it wings;
And even when the traffic roars and rings,
With senses stunned and beaten deaf and blind,
My soul withdraws into itself, and seeks
The peaks and isles and eagles of the mind.

WILFRID GIBSON

THE EAGLE

He hangs between his wings outspread
  Level and still
And bends a narrow golden head,
  Scanning the ground to kill.

Yet as he sails and smoothly swings
  Round the hill-side,
He looks as though from his own wings
  He hung down crucified.

ANDREW YOUNG

BUZZARD

High, high and far away
across the cold blue evening sky
I see death on wings wheel and glide
lazily above the heather:
solitary, beautiful if
only because rare and a symbol
of all that is here and gone,
savage and vulnerable for
a sad irony of reasons.

A delicate image
of a fragile, fleeting canvas
of late-September cloudlessness,
it circles patiently,
dreamily, deceptively over all
the visible and unseen
moments of an evening landscape,
unhurried, unfearing,
unconscious of the intricate
infinity of patterns its mere
existence is creating.

The distance questions me with hills.
I stand under a darkening,
abandoned sky, listening to the heart
that is my only answer, circles
of a single truth behind my eyes,
one among God alone knows
how many roads beneath my feet.

MICHAEL DAUGHERTY

THE ROWAN

When the days were still as deith
    An' ye couldna see the kye,
Tho' ye'd mebbe hear their breith
    I' the mist oot-by;
When I'd mind the lang grey een
    O' the warlock by the hill,
And sit fleggit, like a wean
    Gin a whaup cried shrill;
Tho' the he'rt wad dee in me

At a fitstep on the floor,
There was aye the rowan tree
    Wi' its airm across the door.

But that is far, far past,
    And a'thing's just the same,
But there's a whisper up the blast
    O' a dreid I daurna name;
And the shilpit sun is thin
    As an auld man deein' slow,
And a shade comes creepin' in
    When the fire is fa'in low;
Then I feel the lang een set
    Like a doom upon my heid,
For the warlock's livin yet—
    But the rowan's deid.

                    VIOLET JACOB

MOORBURN IN SPRING

Oft on a dusky night of March, I've watched
The hills aglow with moorburn—crescent lines
Of fiery tongues, leaping along and fast
Up-licking in their round the crackling heath—
Aye snatching impulse from the facing wind,
Wavering, inconstant, and yet pressing on
Fatefully, as a spirit that, conscious
Of its fierce strength, plays free with its resolve,
Yet in the end fails not to gain its goal.
The glowing circle moves, a heart of fire,
Gleaming amid the dim and trailing smoke,
That falls and rises on the fitful air.
Sometimes far east, above the umbered hills,
The moon would rise, large-orbed, and steadily,
In silent power of heavenly influence,
Subdue the shifting, chequered scene of earth,
To perfect oneness with her own clear beauty.
Then I would long, with bounding heart, to be
Away among the fiery-crested hills,
Or wander mid the deepenings of the glens.

                    ANON

IN THE RUT

The summer pipers have flickered
wings off to Africa
their singing spent.
Only a penny robin limps a tune
on a garden wall—
pallid reminder of the lusts of spring,
green season of the birds.

Red autumn belongs to antlered hearts,
to those who would woo
through rain and frost
and snow their passion on the hills.
What toys birds are when stags roar
and roar their month-long rage
of thunderstorm
and waterfall
combined.

There is a remnant of respect
in our plastic observation
of sinewy beast.
He has power to gralloch our past
and remind us of heathery origins
and cave man doubts.
He is our hoary past breathing clouds
of frosty fear into the clean air
we live without.

Stags are the nearest to gods we have,
the nearest to the oldest
stalking hopes of man.
When we hear them bellow on the open strath
we are shut in to centuries
forgotten, rutting the centuries
up to now
till we stand in all-modern pride,
stiff with self-congratulation
at our species.

I would have stayed a stag.

HAMISH BROWN

STAGS

Last night under the stars
The deer came
Down to the road where the white house is;
Black shadows moved in the dark;
Grass ripped as they grazed.

At dawn,
White clouds in blue sky
Were blown
Over the hill above the firs;
Brown ducks
Moved in the shelter of a shed;
And sheep
Pattered over the road to pasture;
But the stags
Left only the cloven print of hooves
In mud beside a stream.

WILLIAM MONTGOMERIE

DEATH OF A HIND

The hind, knocked sprawling by my shot,
rises and weaves about the clearing
like a stage drunk going round a lamppost.
But when I arrive, panting, at her side,
she marshals her straying legs and lines
them up beneath her in a last-ditch effort
at sobriety of direction. It's no use.
Some instincts points her at the fleeing herd
but only her will gallops. While I sweat,
curse and tear at the jammed spent cartridge
she waits, patient now, wielding her dignity.
I clear the jam at last. My bullet,
sawn off at the tip, punches into her.
It unclenches its fist inside her heart.

ALASDAIR MacLEAN

THE ICE HAS SPOKEN

The ice flow cut this valley
and left the loch to lap
the toes of mountain feet
and the older flowing lava
stayed petrified
in waves of silver strata.

Sinking elbow, buttock and heel
in dry yellow sphagnum moss,
I recline at ease watching ants
drag necessity backwards
through the lips of lichened fissures.

Sun and calm;
radiated heat from cliff enclosures;
scarlet cultures thriving
on the rotted rowan stump; the shifting
dragonfly, a shaft of colour,
lifts the scene to an age
of liverworts and mare's-tail.

Reclining on moss,
sinking in self-love and solitude,
the smoke pall of the nearest town
signals remembrance and despair;
what drove me here calls me back:
a city thriving on sweat and sullen love
knit in strange unity,
strange as the impression
I have left on this moss bed
beside the city of ants
in the lichened fissures.

DENIS RIXSON

MOUNTAIN SCULPTURE

hillstones pebbles and boulders
on the mountain slopes
ignored insulted abused despised
scraped scratched kicked and thrown
stumbledagainst slidover and satupon
passedby unnoticed
and yet they are there
to be seen and marvelled at
silent forms of great dignity and loveliness
their infinite variety of shapes and colours
subtle tones of grey and white
clad in robes of lichen and moss
mustard olive russet lime and gold
encrusted rings and spirals
dots and blobs and pinpoints
gems of great beauty
we can so easily miss
these stones are not debris
scattered on the hillside
not the jetsam of the ages
these mountain boulders
have watched the passing seasons
unchanged
through a thousand years
our whole life to them
is but a moment
long after we are gone
the hillstones will be there
the mountain boulders will remain
our stepladder to the high places
our stairway
to the summits

JAMES WILL

STANES

Here on the heich hill.
Thae owrehingin stanes?
Wha say thae canna talk?

Juist rocks. Cauld.
Yellow. Grey. Black.
Broun. E'en reid.
Pittit.
Crumlin. Sayin nocht
that I mind.

Wha says they canna talk?

And the empty waitin yirth
—it talks loud enough?

DUNCAN GLEN

BOG

Half-drying rocks in shades of gray
Moss, be-sundewed bogs
          between
trembling ripples of each stride
          sway
and spread in danger green
          around
where nothing's certain-
          nothing's sound.
Bones of sheep reflect
          unclear
in fluid lochans
          dubh
disturbed by feet in fear
that squeeze the sponge
till land and water
          merge
and rise
    up
      to engulf
        you.

LEEN VOLWERK

MIST

Rain, do not fall
Nor rob this mist at all,
That is my only cell and abbey wall.

Wind, wait to blow
And let the thick mist grow,
That fills the rose-cup with a whiter glow.

Mist, deepen still
And the low valley fill;
You hide but taller trees, a higher hill.

Still, mist, draw close;
These gain by what they lose,
The taller trees and hill, the whiter rose.

All else begone,
And leave me here alone
To tread this mist where earth and sky are one.

ANDREW YOUNG

MIST

'Mist—no sky
Only mist,
Whirling wildly
Weirdly capering
Driven up
Through gullies
On the hollow wind.
Densely thickening
Thinning briefly,
Capricious mist
Twisting silently;
Sinuous grey
Symbiosis.
Cold fingered vapour,
Vision of rocks and
Stones, disturbing;
Creating a new dimension.

Time and distance
Have no meaning
In the uneasy waste;
Horizonless.
A tiny needle
Points direction
Takes command.
Boots plod on
Up and down,
Across and down,
Down the bleak terrain,
Until below the
Swirling hem
of the grey dervish
The valley floor appears.

GILL MAN

KYTHANS

cannily
  the mists smoor
  hale mountain waas
  turn peerie craigs tae
  inaccessible pinnacles
  an sheddaes tae
  bleezan bogles.

sweirt, laith,
  the mists skail,
  an whan they dae
  the fuffs,
  ahent the riggs,
  roun the pinnacles
  mak kythans.

STEWART McGAVIN

CLOUDS AND CLAY

Between the cloud and the ground
a harmony is seen, as turbulence
shapes the hill again in air.

These gunmetal greys and whites
indicate the swollen earth below,
where basic rock soars in an upcurrent.

The hill is a wellbent shoulder
to toll the clouds like bells:
hemispheres peal in set carillon.

The hills, the clouds make chords
—until a wind veer scatters them,
sets notes ajar, breathes on the looking-glass.

The country's image in the atmosphere
flies in pieces. At least, only one man's bearing
is left to guide away the shape of the land's spirit.

For Scotland is spur hills and long hollows
and in that hollow mould she cast him
to be her clay in ideal conformation.

VALERIE GILLIES

FEBRUARY THAW

About us in white mist, ptarmigan
Scold, and hopefully; below,
Bottoming a punctured corrie,
Lochs lie black against the snow.

But here: axes vanish, ropes
Bedraggle, each new step's one huge
Considered extrication, while
The next's beyond all thought. . . . A refuge

In no thought. For thoughts, you know,
Deceive us. Just now they could bring
Some beneath an avalanche;
Others, one day nearer spring.

G. J. F. DUTTON

SPATE IN WINTER MIDNIGHT

The streams fall down and through the darkness bear
Such wild and shaking hair.
Such looks beyond a cool surmise.
Such lamentable uproar from night skies
As turn the owl from honey of blood and make
Great stags stand still to hear the darkness shake.

Through Troys of bracken and Babel towers of rocks
Shrinks now the looting fox.
Fearful to touch the thudding ground
And flattened to it by the mastering sound.
And roebuck stilt and leap sideways; their skin
Twitches like water on the fear within.

Black hills are slashed white with this falling grace
Whose violence buckles space
To a sheet-iron thunder. This
Is noise made universe, whose still centre is
Where the cold adder sleeps in his small bed.
Curled neatly round his neat and evil head.

NORMAN MacCAIG

VIEW FROM MY WINDOW

The scourge of wind first, to flay
the last layer of vegetation from the hills,
then this deluge, obliterating wind and hills,
the eye going out from the ark and returning.

A bleak, inhuman, fearful landscape:
something to roll up and stow in my mind
against those odd moments of happiness.

ALASDAIR MacLEAN

A HINT O' SNAW

The fleur has fa'en:
The bird has gaen:
In stibble fields
Glint stane and stane.

A swurl o' leaves
In the cauld blast;
And on the brae
A flick o' frost:

Look furth, look furth,
And far awa:
On the high hills
A hint o' snaw.

WILLIAM SOUTAR

DISCOMFORT IN HIGH PLACES

Slopping like sphagnum, battered, baptised in cloud,
A leak in every crevice of the soul,
Bones would be warmer bundled in a hole:
White rainstorms beat the mountain's barren head.

Moses was not hauled high on such a day.
All beasts go down, the ravens dive from sight
When the skies open and the floods fall out
And hills are busy sweeping themselves away.

Mist hides the edge of nowhere, which is close.
Miss a short step, and the skied body's fall
Flips a few stones that drop like a burst shell.
Through steaming gullies burns jump the rockface.

Below the mist, down by the salt loch shore
A white rose streams at the end of a wild stalk.
Wind clouts shut doors. What news is there to hawk
Of turbulence, water and everlasting air?

SYDNEY TREMAYNE

NIGHT UP THERE

The moon is down,
But leaves a glow
Of gold, diffused from yon broad cloud
Below the brightest star.
Now sleeps the mountain, every promontory,
Ravine and crag, and crest of drifted snow.

We labour still,
O'er an abyss,
Benumbed, on the wan, stubborn ice
Forming our fragile steps,
And pause for utter weariness, to glance
From gloom above into the night below.

So black a depth!
The ridges close;
The cliff shuts out the very stars.
The snow runs hissing past.
The noise of the mad torrent in the vale
Is faint indeed—and how the dawn delays!

G. D. VALENTINE

MOUNTAIN VIGIL

I thought the dawn would flush to sudden glory—
It came pale of face.
I knew only
It grew slowly
Out of chill space.

I thought there might have been some revelation,
A glimpse beyond the known.
I sensed nothing
But mist brushing
Over grey stone.

I thought my vigil had been ill rewarded.
It found me unprepared,
The full measure
Of cool pleasure,
The secret shared.

DOUGLAS FRASER

THE WILDERNESS

I came too late to the hills: they were swept bare
Winters before I was born of song and story,
Of spell or speech with power of oracle or invocation,

The great ash long dead by a roofless house, its branches
  rotten,
The voice of the crows an inarticulate cry,
And from the wells and springs the holy water ebbed
  away.

A child I ran in the wind on a withered moor
Crying out after those great presences who were not there,
Long lost in the forgetfulness of the forgotten.

Only the archaic forms themselves could tell
In sacred speech of hoodie on gray stone, or hawk in air,
Of Eden where the lonely rowan bends over the dark pool.

Yet I have glimpsed the bright mountain behind the
  mountain,
Knowledge under the leaves, tasted the bitter berries red,
Drunk water cold and clear from an inexhaustible hidden
  fountain.

KATHLEEN RAINE

HILLS

Leisure hills, motorway connected.
Fashioned ski-ing hills, quality inspected.
Hills with plastic huts erected.
Hills where economic gain's detected.
Hills the planning men corrected.
Hills injected, hills dissected.
Hills the TV resurrected;
man-infected, man-protected. Hills
where nuclear waste's expected:

the long identifying Island hills,
the giant-fighting Shetland boulders,
the thrust and relict hills of Torridon,
and Galloway.

Wherever hills grow hard, put them to the test.

ROBIN MUNRO

The Length of the Land

AT KIRK YETHOLM

at kirk yetholm
there is a sign
that points three ways
at the same time

& each arm claims
the same destination.
it is an interesting
place to begin in.

DAVE CALDER

IN THE CHEVIOTS

A small black wedge, the shepherd
lets distance out of the hills,
turns and grunts at his dogs.
They knot up loops of space,
pulling sheep out of nowhere,
a flounce of waves that pour into
seething fanks of grey foam.

Coats of thick hill mist
trailed with tangled twigs and bracken
peel off stuck-out legs
one by one, and sheared strips
are stuffed in bags. Or sheep, thinned
in a splashing yellow trough of bleat
from which they stagger, shake down
their hurt, diminished dignity,
then, following their own baas, run
to where they left their nibbled journey.

The helpers' van unrattles the valley;
the dogs let space go free;
the shepherd strolls loosely home.

Distance re-inflates the hills.

MAURICE LINDSAY

ST MARY'S LOCH

The wind is blowing harshly on the lake.
The snow-patched mountains glimmer through the night.
Winter, too long usurping, needs must make
Some ragged show of sovereignty on each height.
Lambs shiver underneath the freezing sky.
The swallows come not. All the land is gray,
And spring forgotten. Only the curlew's cry
Laments the ancient wealth and peace of May.

So in my spirit belated winter reigns.
The loveliness of self-sufficing things,
The sacred calm of thought, love's quickening pains—
Can these have ever been? Remembrance brings
But phantom suns, too pale and thin to thaw
A heart still prisoned in the frost of war.

GEOFFREY FABER

SHADOWS AMONG THE ETTRICK HILLS

There are always shadows among the hills.
When day dawns, they move down and hide
themselves
In buildings, woods, and under trees and bushes,
Or stretch along old walls, as they were fallen.
When evening comes, they venture forth and wait.
As cold light shines, they spread themselves about,
Broad on the slopes and deep in ugly clefts,
Stark on glittering snow, stone-shaped 'mid graves,
A pall, pierced by pointed lights of clear stars.
Where slow mist creeps, they steal back stealthily;
Anon drive dark and strong on sunny heights,
Telling the higher pageantry of clouds
Aloft in state, moving in majesty.
Again they cling around a silver lining
Under nimbus. By night, in quiet places
As fine mist falls, one coming late, alone,
Grasping his lantern, beholds a giant
Stepping with him in the mist, and hurries
Home to the light that floods the open door.

WILLIAM ADDISON

48

ON ELLSON FELL

The Solway wind
Cavorting in throwe the Ewes Doors
Coosts white clouds afore it:
An the sun etches
Its ain picturs o licht and shadow
On the braid face o Tudhope.

Aneth my feet
The heather lifts its brash tang
An the cotton grass nods in quiet converse
Wi the scarlet cloudberries
Clustering in shy conclave
In the soggy turf.

Line upon line
Stand the distant heichts, traced oot
In purple and blue and grey.
The far streak o siller in the sand:
An nerr at hand only the sheeps' cry
An the burn's soft bicker.

Alang the turnpike road
The restless traffic scuttles bye Mosspaul,
Nor whence ken I, nor whither
But doun in Penangus Hope
A clocks hae stoppit an the world is still,
Still in the quiet o the hills.

WILLIAM LANDLES

GREY GALLOWAY

The years go by, and still both moor and mount
  Wear their memorials of a sterner day:
Here age and death are held of no account,
  The moors have led the centuries astray,
And deep life breaks in me a sudden fount,
  Silent as light in old grey Galloway.

THOMAS S. CAIRNCROSS

APPRENTICES

Once, in the burning age
of flowing stone,
the Devil's old dark toffee overflowed,
and these rocks set
and made Mulwharchar, granite.

The topsoil in our name was grazed and forested,
but never the veins, never the inner self.

It is the inner hills they'd enter now,
his plundering apprentices
of the burning brain.
They'll hide their own pain in the earth,
uranium their power, taste of today
in every atom.

The apprentices are practising.
Not long now, they mutter,
meantime probe.
Not that long to go
And testing.

ROBIN MUNRO

REMEMBERED MELODY
(from *Twilight on Tweed*)

Three crests against the saffron sky,
   Beyond the purple plain,
The dear remembered melody
   Of Tweed once more again.

Twilight, and Tweed, and Eildon Hill,
   Fair and thrice fair you be;
You tell me that the voice is still
   That should have welcomed me.

ANDREW LANG

A BORDER BURN

(from *Epistle to Tammus*)

Ah, Tam! gie me a Border burn
That canna rin without a turn,
And wi' its bonnie babble fills
The glens amang oor native hills.
How men that ance have ken'd aboot it
Can leeve their after lives without it,
I canna tell, for day and nicht
It comes unca'd-for to my sicht.
I see't this moment, plain as day,
As it comes bickerin' o'er the brae,
Atween the clumps o' purple heather,
Glistenin' in the summer weather,
Syne divin' in below the grun',
Where, hidden frae the sicht and sun,
It gibbers like a deid man's ghost
That clamours for the licht it's lost,
Till oot again the loupin' limmer
Comes dancin' doon through shine and shimmer
At headlang pace, till wi' a jaw
It jumps the rocky waterfa',
And cuts sic cantrips in the air,
The picture-pentin' man's despair;
A rountree bus' oot o'er the tap o't,
A glassy pule to kep the lap o't,
While on the brink the blue harebell
Keeks o'er tae see its bonnie sel',
And sittin' chirpin' a' its lane
A water-waggy on a stane.
Ay, penter lad, thraw to the wund
Your canvas, this is holy grund:
Wi' a' its highest airt acheevin',
The picter's deed, and this is leevin'.

J. B. SELKIRK

IF I WERE OLD

If I were old, a broken man and blind,
And one should lead me to Mid-Eildon's crest,
And leave me there a little time to rest
Sharing the hilltop with the Border wind,
The whispering heather, and the curlew's cry,
I know the blind dark could not be so deep,
So cruel and so clinging, but that I
Should see the sunlit curve of Cheviot's steep
Rise blue and friendly on the distant sky!
    There is no darkness—God! there cannot be—
So heavy as to curtain from my sight
The beauty of those Border slopes that lie
Far south before me, and a love-found light
Would shine upon the slow Tweed loitering by
With gift of song and silver to the sea!—
No dark can ever hide this dear loved land from me.

WILL H. OGILVIE

A BORDER FORECAST

Auld Hamish knapped his whunstane chips,
    As roun the gable end
A toff cam in wi bulgin pack
    And dumped it in the pend.
'I say, I'm making for the hills
    To trace the drove road south.
D'you think the weather will keep fine?'
    Auld Hamish wiped his mouth;

'Ah, weel, my man, I dinna doot,
    Ye'll meet a canny drowe,
And aiblins a bit seepin smirr
    Afore the day is throwe.
It could be the odd thunner plump
    Will lowse a pickle water,
But still an on, ye'll no, I trow,
    Be fashed wi goustin blatter.'

Owre at the Snoot, the sun gaed doon
    As that bedraigled hiker
Was wringin oot his socks and sark
    Wi wry thochts o the dyker!

WILLIAM LANDLES

LEAP IN THE SMOKE
(from *From the Pentlands*)

Leap in the smoke, immortal, free,
Where shines yon morning fringe of sea.

I turn;—how still the moorlands lie,
Sleep-locked beneath the awakening sky!
The film of morn is silver-grey
On the young heather, and away,
Dim, distant, set in ribs of hill,
Green glens are shining, stream and mill,
Clachan and kirk and garden-ground,
All silent in the hush profound
Which haunts alone the hills' recess,
The antique home of quietness.
Nor to the folk can piper play
The tune of 'Hills and Far Away,'
For they are with them. Morn can fire
No peaks of weary heart's desire,
Nor the red sunset flame behind
Some ancient ridge of longing mind.
For Arcady is here, around,
In lilt of stream, in the clear sound
Of lark and moorbird, in the bold
Gay glamour of the evening gold.
And so the wheel of seasons moves
To kirk and market, to mild loves
And modest hates, and still the sight
Of brown kind faces, and when night
Draws dark around with age and fear
Theirs is the simple hope to cheer.—
A land of peace where lost romance
And ghostly shine of helm and lance
Still dwell by castled scarp and lea
And the lost homes of chivalry,
And the good fairy folk, my dear,
Who speak for cunning souls to hear,
In crook of glen and bower of hill
Sing of the Happy Ages still.

O Thou to whom man's heart is known,
Grant me my morning orison.
Grant me the rover's path—to see
The dawn arise, the daylight flee,
In the far wastes of sand and sun!

Grant me with venturous heart to run
On the old highway, where in pain
And ecstasy man strives amain,
Outstrips his fellows, or, too weak,
Finds the great rest that wanderers seek!
Grant me the joy of wind and brine,
The zest of food, the taste of wine,
The fighter's strength, the echoing strife,
The high tumultuous lists of life—
May I ne'er lag, nor hapless fall,
Nor weary at the battle-call! . . .
But when the even brings surcease,
Grant me the happy moorland peace;
That in my heart's depth ever lie
That ancient land of heath and sky,
Where the old rhymes and stories fall
In kindly, soothing pastoral.
There in the hills sweet silence lies,
And Death himself wears friendly guise;
There be my lot, my twilight stage,
Dear city of my pilgrimage.

JOHN BUCHAN

THE OCHIL HILLS

What hills are like the Ochil hills?
—There's nane sae green tho' grander.
What rills are like the Ochil rills?
Nane, nane on earth that wander.

ANON
Based on Hugh Haliburton

THE TWINKLING EARN
(from *Winter in Strathearn*)

The twinkling Earn, like a blade in the snow,
The low hills scalloped against the hill,
The high hills leaping upon the low,
And the amber wine in the cup of the sky,
With the white world creaming over the rim . . .

JOHN DAVIDSON

THE GEAN TREES

I mind, when I dream at nicht,
Whaur the bonnie Sidlaws stand
Wi' their feet on the dark'nin' land
And their heids i' the licht;
And the thochts o' youth roll back
Like wreaths frae the hillside track
In the Vale of Strathmore;
And the autumn leaves are turnin'
And the flame o' the gean trees burnin'
Roond the white hoose door.

Aye me, when spring cam' green
And May-month decked the shaws
There was scarce a blink o' the wa's
For the flower o' the gean;
But when the hills were blue
Ye could see them glintin' through
And the sun i' the lift;
And the flower o' the gean trees fa'in'
Was like pairls frae the branches snawin'
In a lang white drift.

Thae trees are fair and gay
When May-month's in her prime,
But I'm thrawn wi' the blasts o' time
And my heid's white as they;
But an auld man aye thinks lang
O' the haughs he played amang
In his braw youth-tide;
And there's ane that aye keeps yearnin'
For a hoose whaur the leaves are turnin'
And the flame o' the gean tree burnin'
By the Sidlaws' side.

VIOLET JACOB

ANE TO ANITHER

(to Phil and Gill and Benjamin)

i LUVE

I've aye been keen on the heich hills.
It was naitural I took you, my luve, to the hills.

You saw nae reason for them,
or us, being
there. Glaur and wet and mair wet in burns
to be crossed. Wund and cauld
and caulder and wundier at the tap. And mist
and ae fit in front o the ither
for langer than you'd thocht possible.
I was the deil and wud wi' it
—and ne'er again!

But come the sun and days by the burn
heich on the hill. I'll ne'er forget
the lawn-like gress
in a giant's airmchair o rock by the langest linn.
And your first real tap. The view o the lans ablow
and the peaks and the lochs to the West,
I see you there still
silent, apairt and yet us thegither
beautiful.

I've lang wondered if God felt
like me or you like
God.

I've aye been interestit in God!

ii HIGH SUMMER

Mad in the midday sun I hae sclimed to the tap.

No the rock faces o Glencoe
or Nevis or the Cuillins
but a steep gressy hill
that's landit me on this endless plateau.

I hae looked for a hole to hide in
or stane to lie unner
but there's nae escape frae the sun.
I hae thochts on the Foreign Legion
as I feel my tongue growe thick.

I'm flet on my back ablow a wee stane
and the blue sky growes paler
And I sink on and on and doun and doun.
My heid spins
afore the eternity o space.
Is God mebbe out there efter aa?

I shout to the sky and the toom space.
The word is there
manifestin me to mysel if no to the warld
like God and His Logos.

'It is the universal principle of aathing in
    particular,
o onything that has being'
I quote to mysel
aye bein interestit in God.

I stare again into the sky
and feel vertigo
wi a mountain plateau streetchin for miles
on aa sides. I think on the Ane
that transcends
and turn to face the gress.

Wi shut een I think on the thickness o this hill.
I see the eternal ground lookin at
itsel. God made manifest for Himsel.

Is there nae escape frae God on this hill?
I think on Saul on that hot road to Damascus

and hae intuitions o my sel on this hill
and o God's haund on my shoulder.

I turn back to the sky
and there's a laverock risin and faain
for real
ayont ony dout
—in my mind!

DUNCAN GLEN

INVERSNAID

This darksome burn, horseback brown,
His rollrock highroad roaring down,
In coop and in comb the fleece of his foam
Flutes and low to the lake falls home.

A windpuff-bonnet of fawn-froth
Turns and twindles over the broth
Of a pool so pitchblack, fell-frowning,
It rounds and rounds Despair to drowning.

Degged with dew, dappled with dew
Are the groins of the braes that the brook treads through,
Wiry heathpacks, flitches of fern,
And the beadbonny ash that sits over the burn.

What would the world be, once bereft
Of wet and of wildness? Let them be left,
O let them be left, wildness and wet;
Long live the weeds and the wilderness yet.

GERARD MANLEY HOPKINS

THERE IS SNOWDRIFT ON THE MOUNTAIN

There is snowdrift on the mountain, there is spindrift on the bay
And dimness in Glen Orchy and dampness in Glen Strae
There once was light in Coire Glas but now it is away
    O Donacha Ban!

It isn't new on Cruachan to stump it thro' the snow
The mistiness of Drochit Glas I've seen it long ago
And when will it be blue again is what I want to know,
    O Donacha Ban!

The cruelties of Cruachan they have been known before
And long it is and difficult their nature to explore
And very little better on Ben Lui or Ben More
    O Donacha Ban!

And very hard on strangers to lead them with your song
Concerning all the glories to Loch Awe that belong:
O goodly is the tune, but the facts a little wrong,
   O Donacha Ban!

But the tune sounds yet, and it sounds all day,
O Donacha Ban nan Oran, and the curlews say
Coming over by Ben Buy they have word of May,
   O Donacha Ban!

W. P. KER

WINTER CLIMB

Lost in the white world
Of whirling snow,
Held in the giant grip
Of the full-bodied wind,
Suspended; in levitation,
Floating along the ridge
So wondrously corniced.

Like a cathedral, the fluted
Snow-shapes rise up
In the wind-whipped mist,
And eerily spicules writhe
Across the frozen surface
Of the ridge, like diaphanous
Snakes, hissing all about.

Music, a giant organ sounds
And splendid notes hurl with
The spindrift over the spiny ridge.
No cacophony this, for harmony
Is in the song of the wind-sped
Snow on snow. Dissonance
Is far below, where man is.

    BEINN EUNAICH

SNOW CRYSTALS ON
MEALL GLAS

There are moments
of fierce frustration
on the hills.
seconds
of such deep harmony
that all the world stands still.
those times which seem
like snowflakes
tangible
—yet melt within one's grasp.

Lacking camera or paints
one gropes for words
which, sterile,
merely mock reality
instead of making
what is perfect
last.

Like shifting images
elusive,
a kaleidoscope
of scenes:
      fantasy in feathers
      fine crystals
      freaks of wind
      fantasia of movement
      frozen
      like a symphony of sounds
      into a chord,
      music arrested into notes;
      crystals
      caught in flight
      like fleeting shadows
      by a camera;
      or thoughts, so rarely
      captured
      in unique and perfect words.

—Tropical plants
grass, frozen in weird and drooping shapes;
—Swans, their wings outstretched
grown from a million darts
of hardened snow,
thrown with beautiful aim
against a stone;
—Ferns in perfect symmetry
brittle to the touch.

Intensely
living patterns
each one perfection
for this brief impermanence:
Nature's philosophy
in the snow.

ELIZABETH A. WILSON

UNDER CREAG MHOR

A lizard fidgets in the sun
That stuns it. Inchlong
And perfect, agile among
Pebbles, it purls its reflection

In crinkling pools. Neither
Freak nor fossil but something
Of each, legends clang
In its speck of a brain, roar

It down at no notice through brown
Peat juice, through mire
Of yellow bogland to where
It discovers its origin.

The bracken scurrs of Creag Mhor,
Pleated with clear water,
No longer house dinosaur
And plated myth. But far

Down, in the cool bright
Element of lizard's tiny
Being, in its ancient eye,
Such monsters huddle yet.

STEWART CONN

FOR SUMMER'S HERE

The road that leads to Rannoch is the gangrel's royal way,
But Ben Doran is to climb, with Stob Gour and Inverveigh;
It taigles us round Tulla, where the red deer have their home
And the salmon flash like silver where the broken waters foam.

The back was made for bundles and the oxter for the pipes
So steep the withie, draw the door, and turn the rusty key;
For summer's here and everywhere there's music in the air,
The waups are on the heather and the white birds on the sea!

RATCLIFFE BARNETT

ONE OF THE MANY DAYS

I never saw more frogs
than once at the back of Ben Dorain.
Joseph-coated, they ambled and jumped
in the sweet marsh grass
like coloured ideas.

The river ran glass in the sun.
I waded in the jocular water
of Loch Lyon. A parcel of hinds
gave the V-sign with their ears, then
ran off and off till they were
cantering crumbs. I watched
a whole long day
release its miracles.

But clearest of all I remember
the Joseph-coated frogs
amiably ambling or
jumping into the air—like
coloured ideas
tinily considering
the huge concept of Ben Dorain.

NORMAN MacCAIG

ON BEN DORAIN
(from *Last Farewell to the Hills*)

Yestreen I stood on Ben Dorain, and paced its dark-
grey path,
Was there a hill I did not know—a glen or grassy
strath?
O gladly in the times of old I trod that glorious
ground,
And the white dawn melted in the sun, and the red-
deer cried around.

How finely swept the noble deer across the morning
hill,
While fearless played the calf and hind beside the
running rill;
I heard the black and red cock crow, and the bellowing
of the deer—
I think those are the sweetest sounds that man at
dawn may hear.

O wildly, as the bright day gleamed, I climbed the
mountain's breast,
And when I to my home returned, the sun was in the
west;
'Twas health and strength, 'twas life and joy, to wander
freely there,
To drink at the fresh mountain stream, to breathe the
mountain air.

. . .

Yestreen I wandered in the glen. What thoughts were
in my head!
There had I walked with friends of yore—where are
those dear ones fled?
I looked and looked; where'er I looked was naught
but sheep, sheep, sheep.
A woeful change was in the hill. World, thy deceit
was deep.

Farewell, ye forests of the heath, hills where the
  bright day gleams,
Farewell, ye grassy dells, farewell, ye springs and
  leaping streams,
Farewell, ye mighty solitudes, where once I loved to
  dwell—
Scenes of my spring-time and its joys—for ever fare
  you well.

DUNCAN BAN MACINTYRE

As Duncan Ban Macintyre's 'Ben Dorain' runs to some hundreds
of stanzas and is difficult to select from, these are a few of the
stanzas this illiterate genius 'wrote' near the end of his life,
translated last century by Robert Buchanan. The best modern
translation of the full poem has been made by Iain Crichton Smith
(*Akros* 1969).

DEER AT THE ROADSIDE
(from *Deer on the High Hills—A Meditation*)

Yesterday three deer stood at the roadside.
It was icy January and there they were
like debutantes on a smooth ballroom floor.

They stared at us out of that French
arrogant atmosphere, like Louis the Sixteenth
sustained in twilight on a marble plinth.

They wore the inhuman look of aristocrats
before a revolution comes, and the people
blaspheme the holy bells in the high steeple.

So were these deer, balanced on delicate logic,
till suddenly they broke from us and went
outraged and sniffing into the dark wind.

Difficult to say where they go to
in the harsh weather when the mountains stand
like judging elders, tall on either hand.

Except that they know the ice is breaking now.
They take to the hills pursued by darkness and lie
beneath the starry metaphysical sky.

Sometimes in a savage winter they'll come down
and beg like fallen nobles for their bread.
They'd rather live in poverty than be dead.

Nevertheless there's something dangerous
in a deer's head. He might suddenly open your belly
with his bitter antlers to the barren sky.

Especially in winter when tormented
by lonliness they descend to this road
with great bounding leaps like the mind of God.

IAIN CRICHTON SMITH

ENVOY

On Meall nan Con, the Peak of the Dogs,
two skeletons of stags lie head to head,
both royals, their antlers laced together.

I watched the fight that led to this
and watched without complaint
the long death that followed it.

A hummel served the hinds that year
whose strength was all between his legs,
not growing from his skull in antique patterns.

It is with diffidence I note their struggle.
A still more ancient craft they studied,
each bonded to the master opposite.

The deer is noble, a Roman animal.
I remember how the grass was trampled
and how finally they loved each other.

ALASDAIR MacLEAN

PASSIN BEN DORAIN

(from *At the Heich Kirk-yaird*)

The bens camp by the road-side
I see their tents pitcht forby
on the sky-line hyne awa.

The totty cars birr north,
an assembly line on holiday.

Or park.
And fowk get oot and streetch themsels
or wire in to their sandwiches,
tak the view in
and read the news o the warld.

It's aa cheenged Duncan Ban;
the aixed wuds and the thinned deer
and the fowk that took their tongue somewey else.
Aye, it fair gies the toomness
mair elba-room.

wha's listenin?
Whit's there to listen till?

The muckle lug o the glen
is cockit still for a music furder back,
Moladh Ben Dorain,
a pibroch o a mountain,
and you
makkin it wi praise.

The road's a spate o metal.
Aa I can dae
is to pint in homage to the poem
as we drave by its theme and variations.

ALASTAIR MACKIE

RANNOCH MOOR

As the sun, its globe compressed in
The mist-sprayed air, sinks lidless down
Grey-backed hoodies pick from bleached bones
The flesh of rabbits, decaying.
Black raven flaps its timid way
From such gregarious neighbours.

Near-treeless plateau, mountain-high
With but the one storm-stunted pine,
Still brushes the clouds from the sky.

Long, across the rush-strewn moors, the
Shadows of the glacial drumlins.
Some high about the lonely road,
Some low, half-hidden in the glass
Of shallow pools unrunnelled by
The meanders of streamlets.

As the sun, its globe compressed in
The mist-sprayed air, sinks lidless down.

MALCOLM MacGREGOR

RANNOCH, BY GLENCOE

Here the crow starves, here the patient stag
Breeds for the rifle. Between the soft moor
And the soft sky, scarcely room
To leap or soar. Substance crumbles, in the thin air
Moon cold or moon hot. The road winds in
Listlessness of ancient war,
Languor of broken steel,
Clamour of confused wrong, apt
In silence. Memory is strong
Beyond the bone. Pride snapped,
Shadow of pride is long, in the long pass
No concurrence of bone.

T. S. ELIOT

BUACHAILLE ETIVE MOR AND BUACHAILLE ETIVE BEAG

Those two bad shepherds, hunched above their sheep,
Dreaming of blood and pain and the long sleep
In their too certain circumstance of when:
Two black shepherds and myself and the Glen.

If you speak ill of the shepherds, speak it low;
Wait for the winter, they say, wait for the snow,
Wait for the night of the Campbells, the day of the fox,
The frayed rope and the boot that slips on the rocks.

NAOMI MITCHISON

GLENCOE

The star-crowned cliffs seem hinged upon the sky,
The clouds are floating rags across them curled,
They open to us like the gates of God
Cloven in the last great wall of all the world.

I looked, and saw the valley of my soul
Where naked crests fight to achieve the skies,
Where no grain grows nor wine, no fruitful thing,
Only big words and starry blasphemies.

But you have clothed with mercy like a moss
The barren violence of its primal wars,
Sterile though they be and void of rule,
You know my shapeless crags have loved the stars.

How shall I thank you, O courageous heart,
That of this wasteful world you had no fear;
But bade it blossom in clear faith and sent
Your fair flower-feeding rivers: even as here.

The peat burns brimming from their cups of stone
Glow brown and blood-red down the vast decline
As if Christ stood on yonder clouded peak
And turned its thousand waters into wine.

G. K. CHESTERTON

68

THE LOST VALLEY

Winding, winding,
Upwards to Shangri-La
Shake off the bindings,
Follow your star.
Ever ascending
Winding,
Winding,
Past trees,
Bushes, rocky eaves.
Feel the breeze through
Leaves, golden brown
In the
Sun.

Touch,
Touch, touch
The leaves, have
Fun, while Glencoe's
Sisters brooding spell
Is spun
Spun
Spun
Spun by
Cataracts from forgotten
Streams, Scotland's magic moments
Bidean's unknown dreams.

High above
Rising
Rising
Falling, circling
A golden eagle
Stalling against smooth rock
Soars in the
Azure world
Circling,
Regal,
Wings unfurled.

Giant boulders pass
Whilst stones and debris mass
To bar your
Way, but
Pass,
Pass,
Pass over
The massed mound
To an enchanted world
Lush meadows, round
Which are
Mountains,
Mountains,
Mountains curled
In awesome splendour.
A lonely paradise unfurled.
Mundane world afar
We've found
Shangri-La.

GORDON J. GADSBY

BIDEAN NAM BIAN

Here it begins, the day we shall not forget,
With a change of wind at dawn. The rain drips
Still from the slates, but across the moor
The pearly light spreads, and, facing the sun,
The crags appear, slowly, plane behind plane
Shaping the dark cone, with punctuation
Of solid white left as the grey recedes.
O morning freshness of heart!
Down the road the air sings, the water sings
Beside us; but up on Beinn Fhada,
Where the angle eases, and snowdrifts
Succeed the rough wet outcrops,
There is only the music of breath and footfall.
Below, the bright brown pass still holds the sun;
Away to westward, our mountain
Spreads its limbs wide under pale shadow,
And beyond is the green Arctic light
Over the sea; to the north the high wildernesses
Regard us; and from Glen Etive pours the covering cloud.

Out of the mist the three white ridges converge,
Rise to the summit's blunted pyramid.
Curious men, truth-lovers, closely questioning,
Peering, measuring, lifetime after lifetime,
Learn how these shapes were carved
By air and water in the sun's hand.
But who shall say what powers shaped us three,
Directed us inward from what distances,
Over what peaks and gaps, through obscurity
To make this perfect form, which stands
Beautiful and gracious now, overlooking
A wider territory than Argyll?

You know, standing with me on the snow crest—
You know, mountaineers, on other hills
Instructed—you know, music makers,
Choosing out of the infinite range of sounds
Created and dying the elements of eternal
Patterns—how the obvious harmony
By sudden unwilled comprehension becomes
Part of a harmony of higher order,
The soul gains freedom in a new dimension.
So was our triad seized,
Merged in the huge chord of the winter hills,
Our human love given its place in Love,
Our private design made suddenly significant
In the moment's vision of the Idea
Which is our origin, our life, our goal,
The Good.

Shine in us, shine,
When we descend again into the world of shadows.

The smooth grey road rises, falls, rises again,
From the throat of the pass to the bridge, from the bridge to
    the moor,
And the thick night covers
Bog and river and rough hills and sky.
Beside us the water sings, the air sings:
O blessed tiredness, blessed content!
Peace falls from the unseen crags; and ahead,
High ahead, is a gleam of yellow light
Where a door will open, to lamps and a smoky fire,
And love declared again in the breaking of bread,
And the day complete that we shall remember.

A. M. DOBSON

ON THE CROUN O BIDEAN

Aince on the croun o Bidean,
Wi a watery sun in the wast,
I saw a wraith on the rouk there
That gied me the key at last.

For there on the mist ablow me
As I stude on the heichmaist cairn,
I saw a ghaistly shadow
That gart me gowp like a bairn.

A shadow lang-shankit and ugsome,
But happt in a bruch sae braw
That aside it the weather-gaw's colours
Seemed dowf as the underfit snaw.

That shadow lang-shankit and ugsome
Was like 'Arctic reek' on the sea.
I midged; and the shadow moved wi me
And I kent that the shadow was me.

I raxt out my ice-aix abune me
And aa was as clear as day.
I saw mysel as Skarphedinn
As he lap owre the Fleet to the fray.

I saw mysel as Skarphedinn
And I kent that the hills were mine
Sin the blude of my Norse forebears
Melled the mountain dew and the brine.

                    J. K. ANNAND

CORRIES

Corries are like pots of transmutation,
Eerie vessels, magic cauldrons
Of ancient tales; boiling vapour,
Mist, rain, snow, hail into roots.
Roots of grasses, of flowers, of trees,
(Alpine birch and creeping willow);
Rivers' roots, life sap
Ready for spring.

For fifty years I have loved corries
But have not praised them. Stupid. Dumb.
Feet can worship, eyes can adore,
But words—dear, plaguey, illusive words
Are not to mind when spirit needs them.
There is only the silence of corries.
Maybe a plover's cry.

Yet I have loved them: Coire Lagan
Where once a friend heard alien singing
From deep water, and so was drawn
To the water's edge, in the mist, by the singing,
An won back late, by a friend below.
Perhaps she knew, perhaps now she knows
The corrie's secret—that womb of the hill,
The pot, the depth of life.

Coir'a'Ghrunnda has the wide slabs,
The sun's anvil to beat out eyes
In extreme heat. Coire Mhic Fhearchair
Of the huge shoulders like Norway's sea cliffs
Could swallow most others. Coire Etchachan
Dear and familiar, is studded with cushion pinks
Coral on grey granite. And the little corries,
Coireachan beaga of hundred hillsides
Are for everyday use.

Now if some words after fifty years
Can join in praise, it is praise of deep things,
Springs, streams and water, the hills' own life.

JANET M. SMITH

SCHIEHALLION

Years, long years ago, I read of a death I envied.
A girl climbing alone on this noble mountain
With its glittering quartzite cone,
Was caught in a thunderstorm,
Struck by lightning,
And killed.

She died, high up on the hill
In the lovely spring of her youth,
Under the lightning flash
With the boom of thunder
Echoing round and round.

The rain would be beating the sweet wild scents
From the honeyed heather,
The yellowy lady's-bedstraw, the creeping thyme,
And the tangy mountain grasses.

Rain-cleansed and sained by the scents
She died as quick as the lightning;
And I envied her a death,
So swift, so clean,
At the hand of heaven.

So would I die, thought I
As shortly after I climbed that self-same hill
(Young too, and happy and strong)
On a brilliant day of heat
That shimmered above the heather;
Far off, in the crystal air
Tummel and Rannoch lochs lay silver and blue,
(No pylons yet bestriding their virgin bounds)
And deep in the woods, the Lyon
Was leaping with salmon.
Fortingal slept by its ancient yew,
And windows eyebrowed with thatch.

And though I was happy and young
And hoped to climb many more Munros
In my lovely Scotland,
I saw the prophetic years stretching ahead
When strength would fail and the weight of years
Would drag me down and restrict my urge
To climb to the top of the world.

Now, half a century on,
I lift my aching feet on the city stones.
My heart is heavy with thought of the
Hate in the world,
And the hideous problems wrought
By distrust and greed.
Is Prayer the Answer?

I think of the hills in their pure clean air,
And that man-made clouds of poison
May rest upon them, and us,
Annihilating all;
And I long to reach the crest
Of my earthly life, and gain
Schiehallion.

                    HELEN B. CRUICKSHANK

HAUF-ROADS UP SCHIEHALLION

Well
we were hauf-roads up Schiehallion
and Michael (natch) was well in front
showin off as usual—climbin rocks
when Alasdair
turned around and said
'Whae d'ye think he's efter?
You—or Eileen?'

Well
'And what makes you think' says I
'that he's *efter* either wan o us?
EILEEN—or myself?'
I said.
Alasdair blushed.

'Well' says he 'I aye sort of
thought that Michael sort of
fancied you—only last night I sort of
saw them—
Michael 'n Eileen—sort of
back o the bothy—sort of
havin it away'

Well
I sort of sniffed—held my tongue
Alasdair grinned—and blushed again.

There
we were—hauf-roads up Schiehallion
and Alasdair turned around and said
'Well, that's aaaright!'
I could have spat! Just what in the hell
did he mean by that?

'Michael' says he 'Ye dinnae fancy him?'

Aw naw, I says
Not a bit of it, I says
Couldnae care less, I says
Here I am—HAUF-ROADS UP PIGGIN SCHIEHALLION
Aa for the guid o my health!

DONALD CAMPBELL

LOCH OSSIAN

It was a heat to melt the mountains in,
The basking adder sunned his varnished span
And cooled the burning rock beneath his skin.
The aromatic resin swelled and ran;
Whilst, in the arid timber, tall and still,
Each needle nodded in the larch's shade:
And, bare above its plaid, the shapely hill
Seemed as the sunburnt shoulders of a maid,
Shyly disrobing by the shore alone.
Loch Ossian looked its very loveliest,
With lazing water warm against the stone,
The heron silent in his island nest,
And such a golden langour through the haze
That Summer seemed in love with idle days.

SYD SCROGGIE

BEN ALDER 1963-1977

I came back to where we killed the deer;
(myself, the Cruick and James),
to Ben Alder and the Cam, the Bealach Dubh,
each name rang clear. Myself,
I moved with that old fluency,
the broadland over
and found the Culra, after all these years,
unchanged.
Mountains made me there.

I saw again, those mountain shapes we made,
through stalker's weather
and still, in the land-lock,
some small infinity,
might cause my heart's turning;
those rocks, the burning sky, a memory,
of garrons in the windy distance,
white sails on a green sea.

DES HANNIGAN

NIGHT EXPEDITION FROM
BEN ALDER COTTAGE

High on Ben Alder on wintery night
Where the crusty dome glints in the stars
I walk with the cornice far to my right
And hope to come to the cairn.

This is a peak for a wintery night,
A ptarmigan summit of empty snow.
No moonbeams here—just bright starlight
And the crunch of my boots as I go.

No moon shines from this black night sky
But the white-piled cairn stands ahead,
Seen by the light of stars on high,
Stars in the black and stars on the hill.

The stags aren't roaring by Alder Burn,
The burn is silent, too.
The empty larches crack in turn,
Like frosted sticks on Ericht-side.

Down in the same boot-holes I go,
Half imagined in this starlight.
Plunge and skid and brake in the snow
On the steep trail down to Alder Bay,
Where the cottage chimney still shoots sparks
And the candle we lit casts its ray
From the window across the snow.

ROGER A. REDFERN

SPACE AND TIME

Only a hundred yards, says Bob,
But there are bogs and stones to
dodge,
And it is getting dark as well:
Only a hundred yards to Culra Lodge.

The water's glazing in the pools,
The rocks are glittering with rime;
Only a hundred yards to go,
But not in distance, Syd—in time.

SYD SCROGGIE

STAOINEAG

Above the stream, grunting Staoineag stands,
stones stuck to living stone
at one with rock,
an elbow to the west.
Cold from the corries, wind slaps
        the sheeting hard
and fires the hail, to stot along the corrugations,
        seeking entry.

A sentry
   in the narrow glen she stands defiant,
desperately alone,
   except for coughing sheep and memories
thrown from distant towns
by hillmen who here have bedded down
and briefly called it home.

LEEN VOLWERK

THE HARLOT

Ben Nevis is a mountain
of loveless loveliness.
Like a fat woman she broods,
cold-shouldered of warm romance,
too drunk for gentle kiss.
Love has just scratched her. She reeks
like a discarded garment.

As so many cold hundreds
have pissed against the cairn,
she is soiled through and wet
and weary in her solitude.

Yet it is to this harlot
the generations come—brash boys
to test their nascent lusts,
a giggle that so often has an echoed death.

I have come to hate the bitch.

The sterile heart of her is stone
and her smile is slimy ice.
We should have heeded the kind advice:
Not all snowy frills—or hills—are nice.

HAMISH BROWN

HUT

it is almost too simple
here under the mountain,
snow flying
lightning
and roaring water.

the unwashed plates.
and the weather too obviously bad
to go out.
six men
in a bare room

walking from window
to fire and back again.
each one
identical
but for the others.

simple as
condoning the galaxies,
given the time
what infinite
can help it. white

sheeting the window,
thunder over the flood,
six men
laughing
keeping the fire bright

and if it had happened,
we should have described the avalanche.
boot. splinter
of chair.
somebody else's photograph.

G. J. F. DUTTON

EAGLE

The weather came down from Nevis,
A schiltrom of snow spearmen
Marching across the glen.
We, high on a bare Mamore,
Braced for the blast when
He, above us, slanted into a
Slot of cold air.
Aquila chrysaetos
Poised in his perfection.
For a moment he stopped our world.
Slammed shut all emotion save
Praise to the eagle.
And we did,
Joyfully with eyes and lips.
Then he was gone
Riding easy the teeth of the gale.
Full sail set and rigging singing
He slid round a lee crag.
Gone and away.
But etched on our minds
Forever.

TOM BOWKER

WRITTEN UPON THE TOP OF BEN NEVIS

Read me a lesson, Muse, and speak it loud
  Upon the top of Nevis, blind in mist!
I look into the chasms, and a shroud
  Vapourous doth hide them,—just so much I wist
Mankind do know of hell; I look o'erhead,
  And there is sullen mist,—even so much
Mankind can tell of heaven; mist is spread
  Before the earth, beneath me,—even such,
Even so vague is man's sight of himself!
  Here are the craggy stones beneath my feet,—
Thus much I know that, a poor witless elf,
  I tread on them,—that all my eye doth meet
Is mist and crag, not only on this height,
But in the world of thought and mental might!

JOHN KEATS

CLIMBING ZERO GULLY

There is no cut rock,
but terrified stones
keeping the peace,
unchallenging.

They challenge:
perusing second pitch belay,
scribing snake-backs in the snow,
hard as glacier,

the piton correcting itself
almost self-consciously.
Hand and overhand, they jerk
upwards and on,

absolutely competent, nursed
by Japanese equipment.
On comes a broken night,
bleating, unchallenging.

Rock: screw-faced and water-brained.
They: complete in mountain-power,
stand, chin in hand,
suddenly vigilant.

DAVID J. MORLEY

DRUMOCHTER

Here where the wind skins Drumochter
Where mica glints from the bared rocks
And the uncovered rivers flow
Here under the space of sky
The rounded, hunted shapes of hills
Flee to the horizon.
Brown, tweed-cloaked hunchbacks
They cower as they go
Lean low as they clamber and push
Clumsily jostling for speed.
But the hills are heavy here
Cannot reach and grasp the wind.
Even in haste their pace is slow.
They struggle for speed, for height
And fall heavily like grouse.
Here where the wind skins Drumochter
Only the storm moves fast.

ANNE B. MURRAY

THE BOAR OF BADENOCH AND THE SOW OF ATHOLL

Few have seen the King Selkie and few the grand
Sweep of the wings as the Queen Swan comes to land,
In the long light days of summer when
    florrish is sweet on the bough,
Seeking their island mates between the machair and plough.
But none saw the Boar of Badenoch cover his sow.

Away on the skerry the Selkie nurses his dream,
Far from her shining bridal the Swan has flown.
And the Boar of Badenoch couches, stiff and alone,
Weighted, the ridge of his bristles,
    with scree and heather and stream
For his sow has eaten her pigs and turned into stone.

NAOMI MITCHISON

84

THE ROAD

There are some that love the Border-land and some the Lothians
   wide,
And some would boast the Neuk o' Fife and some the banks o'
   Clyde,
And some are fain for Mull and Skye and all the Western Sea;
But the Road that runs by Atholl will be doing yet for me.

The Road it runs by Atholl and climbs the midmost brae
Where Killiecrankie crowns the pass with golden woods and gay;
There straight and clean 'twas levelled where the Garry runs
   below
By Wade's red-coated soldiery two hundred years ago.

The Road it strikes Dalwhinnie where the mountain tops are grey
And the snow lies in the corries from October until May;
Then down from bleak Ben Alder by Loch Ericht's wind-swept
   shore
It hastes by Dalnaspidal to the howes of Newtonmore.

The Road it runs through Badenoch, and still and on it rings
With the riding of the clansmen and a hundred echoings;
Oh, some they rode for vengeance, and some for gear and gain,
But some for Bonnie Charlie rode and came not home again.

The Road it runs by Alvie—you may linger if you list
To gaze on Ben Muich-Dhuie and the Larig's cap of mist;
There are pines in Rothiemurchus like a gipsy's dusky hair,
There are birch trees on Craigellachie like elfin silver-ware.

The Road it runs to Forres and it leaves the hills behind,
For the roving winds from Morayshire have brought the sea to
   mind;
But still it winds to northward in the twilight of the day,
Where the stars shine down at evening on the bonny haughs
   o' Spey.

Oh, there's some that sing of Yarrow stream, Traquair and
   Manor-side,
And some would pick the Neuk o' Fife and some the banks
   o' Clyde;
And some would choose the Pentlands, Cauldstaneslap to
   Woodhouselee,
But the Road that runs by Atholl will be doing yet for me.

CHRISTINE ORR

BEINN A' GHLO

You are not alone on the mountain.
The deer have been there
and the wildcat pressed his great paws
into the snow you toiled up just now.
The summit cairn of frozen stones
shelters you from sharp wind.
Below the cold dark cloud
clear air shows the black loch
and the far hills, white etched.

Down to the col, up round the corrie;
the hills watch, follow with
their monstrous gaze each move
of foot and axe on snow.
Braigh Coire Cruinn-bhalgain
reached—cold, cold—a storm comes
tearing over Carn nan Gabhar.

You escape, floundering in drifts,
plunging down to pass the snow line,
glissade down grass slippery as ice,
drop like a stone into water
among the resting deer, who
splash up away and vanish.

BILL TULLOCH

LOCHAN

We fluttered from the ridge
Like wounded birds
Looking for the small blue eye
The map had promised
For our resting place.

How tired we were: not with the
Weary tiredness of the city
But with a fine fatigue of footsore miles.

We found our small blue eye,
Unpacked, put up the tent, and made
The first of many brews.
From water we had come—a morning sea
We dipped our toes in; by water
We would sleep, the quiet sun-blessed lochan
Guarded by the ridge, blessed our feet anew.

That long blue day,
The first of eight
Encapsulated everything we sought to find
And never felt to end.

ROGER SMITH

LONG AGO

On Broad Cairn, I remember still,
The knitted boulders (green and cold)
Hang on the shoulders of the hill
Like chain-mail, hammered on of old—
Perdurably it seems. I say
'Remember' for the topaz burns
Have brimmed and spilt, that eagle's day
Is done that, idle, soars and turns,
Engraved in lapis lazuli—
The deerskin stretch of heather-land,
The smoking crag, the drifting sky,
The little loch, the hidden stand
Of aromatic larch below
The breast of Broad Cairn, long ago.

SYD SCROGGIE

CAENLOCHAN

I saw a herd of the wild red deer
In dark Caenlochan Glen.
They scented me, saw me, wheeled and fled,
Splashed through the burn, and upward sped
Into the mists on Monega's head,
And all that was left me then
Was an echoing splash in my startled ear
And a dream that beauty had been near;
Stag, and fawn, and following hind
Vanished and trackless as the wind;
Half a hundred wild things gone—
And dark Caenlochan left alone.

Once, on a long-time vanished night
You opened your mind to me.
Enchanted I looked. One fated word,
Clumsy, not false, I spoke. No herd
Of deer e'er fled so fast, or bird
Sprang from a shaken tree.
So fled your thoughts in panic flight,
Their fastness shrouded from my sight—
The proud, the tender ones, the shy,
Whither no friend or foe might pry;
And beauty glimpsed was swift withdrawn
As startled stag and soft-eyed fawn.

HELEN B. CRUICKSHANK

CHANGE AND IMMUTABILITY

When I went up to Clova glen
And I was in my 'teens
And got there on a bicycle
And lived on bread and beans
And covered twenty miles or so
And got up Dreish and Mayar
The May month oystercatcher flights
Were madly piping there.

When I went up to Clova glen
And I was fifty-five,
And lived on wine and caviare
And had a car to drive.
And managed half a dozen miles
And halfway up the hill
The May month oystercatcher flights
Were madly piping still.

SYD SCROGGIE

FOXGLOVES AND SNOW

Two things have set the world a-twist
And spoiled the music of the spheres;
One is a lovely secret missed,
And one a wrong beyond all tears.

Sweet secret—I shall never know,
Though seas run dry, and suns turn cold,
How many purple foxgloves grow
This summer by the ruined fold.

And—sorry wrong—though roses red
By western waters bloom and fall,
No more I watch the last snows fade
On a dark hill above Glen Doll.

MARION ANGUS

THE PATRIOT

Fecht for Britain? Hoot awa!
For Bonnie Scotland? Imph, man, na!
For Lochnagar? Wi' clook and claw!

J. C. MILNE

BENNACHIE

There's Tap o' Noth, the Buck, Ben Newe,
　　Lonach, Benrinnes, Lochnagar,
Mount Keen, an' mony a Carn I trow
　　That's smored in mist ayont Braemar.
Bauld Ben Muich Dhui towers, until
　　Ben Nevis looms the laird o' a';
But Bennachie! Faith, yon's the hill
　　Rugs at the hairt when ye're awa'!

Schiehallion,—ay, I've heard the name—
　　Ben More, the Ochils, Arthur's Seat,
Tak' them an' a' your hills o' fame
　　Wi' lochans leamin' at their feet;
But set me doon by Gadie side,
　　Or whaur the Glenton lies by Don—
The muir-cock an' the whaup for guide
　　Up Bennachie I'm rivin' on.

Syne on the Mither Tap sae far
　　Win'-cairdit clouds drift by abeen,
An' wast ower Keig stands Callievar
　　Wi' a' the warl' to me, atween.
There's braver mountains ower the sea,
　　An' fairer haughs I've kent, but still
The Vale o' Alford! Bennachie!
　　Yon is the Howe, an' this the Hill!

CHARLES MURRAY

IN LYTHE STRATHDON

Seldom a simmer passed but him an' me
  Amang the hills had some fine cheery days,
  Up Nochtyside or throu' the Cabrach braes,
Doon the Lord's Throat, an' ootower Bennachie;
There wasna mony bare hill-heads onkent to him an' me.

Never nae mair. I wander noo my leen,
  An' he's been beddit lang in far Peronne;
  Here, whaur his forbears lie in lythe Strathdon,
I lay the stag-moss that I pu'ed yestreen—
Laurels fae Lonach, where I range oor auld hill tracks my leen.

CHARLES MURRAY

THE DRUNKEN DEE

The Quoich, the Ey, the Slugain,
The Luibeg forbye,
A' stan the bouse this muckle sous
Makes free wi on his wey.
Aye doon the strath he danders,
Straveiglin like a coo,
Till syne ae nicht he jist scales richt
Intil the ocean, fou.

SYD SCROGGIE

IN PRAISE OF BEN AVON

In loneliness or grief, I treasure yet my friendship with Ben A'an. For she is peaceful as a slow river, and there is no vice in her.

The dappled hind hides in her heather; the blue hare lopes across her shining scree. The oyster-catchers haunt the lily-pool, beside the crumbling cottages of Gairn.

There is black blood in the Calf's Vein, and snow about the knees of Stùc Gharbh Mhór. The slim bog-asphodel among the peat raises her yellow torch to light your way.

You will breathe hard before you reach the top—and harder when you meet the beetle-browed Rockmen who live upon the mountain's crest, and stand in rows, their backs against the wind.

I like the Rockmen. They are so solemn. (No doubt geologists will have a name for them.) To me, they are like weather-beaten faces, uplifted to the candle of the sun.

They do not worry, or try to hide their age. Scarred by the snows and riven by the rain; wise as the wind and silent as the stones; they watch the seasons march across the sky.

They have learned patience with the beetle balanced on the canna-stems at dusk. They see the shadow-patterns flow and fade, and know that all things pass—and come again.

If there be any faery music, they have heard it. They have communed with the rotating stars (and they do not tell what they know).

. . . And they will stand when all of us are gone; with their weird heads pillowed on the clouds, and their unshifting feet rooted forever in the mountain's heart.

BRENDA G. MACROW

BENIGHTED TO THE FOOTHILLS
OF THE CAIRNGORMS

Cauld, cauld is Alnack.
Cauld is the snaw wind and sweet.
The maukin o' Creagan Alnack
Has snaw for meat.

Nae fit gangs ayont Caiplich,
Nae herd in the cranreuch bricht.
The troot o' the water o' Caiplich
Dwells deep the nicht.

On a' the screes, by ilk carn
In the silence nae grouse is heard,
But the eagle abune Geal Charn
Hings like a swerd.

Yon's nae wife's hoose ayont A'an
In the green lift ava.
Yon's the cauld lums o' Ben A'an,
Wha's smeek is snaw.

A' the lang mountains are silent.
Alane doth wild Alnack sing.
The hern, the curlew are silent,
Silent a' thing.

OLIVE FRASER

AT THE SHELTER-STONE

Leaving the snows,
the windy wastes of Etchachan,
we half-glissade
down the soft brae to where
Cairn Gorm comes up to meet us, dizzily
inverted in the dark glass of Loch A'an.

A puff of cloud
clings in the Castle Gate.
Below, the track
threads among headlong boulders flung
from the uncaring heights in some remote
upheaval of the world.

Now rears the Rock
its massive head. The narrow cavern gapes.
Inside, the candles
gutter in the palpitating dark,
Greeted, we drop our axes—stretch
tired limbs, reach fumbling hands to sign the book.

The gusty night
flows round—but here is peace
and none are strangers. One
makes tea for all. Another tends
the candles—shakes fresh heather for a bed.
We sing, tell tales, upon the edge of sleep.

And we are well content
(though many lie on softer beds this night)
with the hard rock, the creeping cold,
the thrumming of the wind—
outside, the vast
calm of the hills beneath a vestal moon.

BRENDA G. MACROW

DOLOMITES

O I gaed furth and far awa to see what I cou'd see,
And loshtie! siccan heichts o' Hills I nivver thocht cou'd be!
I lookit lang and lookit at yon grander Hills afar
Till I fairly tint a' notion o' the Hielan' Hills o' Mar.

'Twis here I cam' and hame again fae yonner faur I'd been,
And day and nicht yon fremmit hills were aye afore ma een!
Till 'Dyod!' thinks I, 'I doot, my lad, ye mebbe micht dae waur
Than tak' a dauner westward to the Hielan' Hills o' Mar.'

Ay, there they were, like brithers, Ben Macdhui, Carn Toul,
Braeriach, Cairngorm—man, a sicht to sair the sowl!
And braid Ben A'an and Beinn a' Bhuird, and yonner Lochnagar,
A' noddin-aul' and neibourlike, the Hielan' Hills o' Mar!

And govie dick! at gloamin-time, maist Hielan' time o' a'!
The young and lordly Dolomites gaed worth and clean awa!
And left a leear thinkin, 'Though ye've traivelled furth and far,
Ye hinna traivelled far'er than the Hielan' Hills o' Mar.'

J. C. MILNE

THE SILENT WALLS
(on Derry Lodge, now unoccupied)

The slender pine skirts walls now silent;
and gaunt, deserted, stones no longer ring
with voices we remember, of mountain days, of joys long gone.
Only the voice of the wind calls, and ghosts remain.

The lone stag grazes near the door now sealed,
where once a welcome warmed the heart and cheered
the climber returning weary, to recall moments on Cairngorm
   heights,
and Derry's walls lured us to rest at journey's end.

No wisp rises from glowing log, and absence
stills the young voice that sang of hill and glen.
The strike of steel on stone has gone; and as we gaze upon
the lodge, we hear only the music of the mountain.

In mind, the walls open to embrace the sounds we knew,
friends return to greet with cheery call, and faces are
    remembered,
and as we tread to snowy height, voices sing again,
and praise the land of silver snow frozen on mossy bed.

IAN STRACHAN

HIGHLAND SHOOTING LODGE

Crouched up beneath a crowd of Grampian hills,
this old house waits to hear the report of guns
crisping the Autumn air, for its rooms again
to warm to the jokes of August-trampling men
roughed by the grasp and snap of salmon gills,
the twisted necks of grouse. But nobody comes.

Only, at times, a shapeless horde of cloud
that shifts about the rocky peaks, creeps down
to lick at gutters soured with rotting leaves,
or rub a shapeless back against cold eaves,
then vanish, thin as breath; the drifting shroud
of everything men once had thought they owned.

MAURICE LINDSAY

THE HILL BURNS

So without sediment
Run the clear burns of my country,
Fiercely pure,
Transparent as light
Gathered into its own unity,
Lucent and without colour;
Or green,

Like clear deeps of air,
Light massed upon itself,
Like the green pinions,
Cleaving the trouble of approaching night,
Shining in their own lucency,
Of the great angels that guarded the Mountain;
Or amber so clear
It might have oozed from the crystal trunk
Of the tree Paradisal,
Symbol of life,
That grows in the presence of God eternally.
And these pure waters
Leap from the adamantine rocks,
The granites and schists
Of my dark and stubborn country.
From gaunt heights they tumble,
Harsh and desolate lands,
The plateau of Braeriach
Where even in July
The cataracts of wind
Crash in the corries with the boom of seas in anger;
And Corrie Etchachan
Down whose precipitous
Narrow defile
Thunder the fragments of rock
Broken by winter storms
From their aboriginal place;
And Muich Dhui's summit,
Rock defiant against frost and the old grinding of ice,
Wet with the cold fury of blinding cloud,
Through which the snow-fields loom up, like ghosts from a world
    of eternal annihilation,
And far below, where the dark waters of Etchachan are wont to
    glint,
An unfathomable void.
Out of these mountains,
Out of the defiant torment of Plutonic rock,
Out of fire, terror, blackness and upheaval,
Leap the clear burns,
Living water,
Like some pure essence of being,
Invisible in itself,
Seen only by its movement.

NAN SHEPHERD

WIND

The dark is no more than a blanket,
Soft and safe, or a curtain hung
Silver on the moonlit night.
It is the invisible in the void we fear,
It is that stranger, unpredictable,
That gives this fright.

Snow pillows down, like children laughing,
A gentle delight, dancing
A pleasant hour.
It is the devil dance, Dervish dance, we fear.
The enemy supreme, who drowns the world in white
Satins of smothering power.

Stir up the fire lad! By nature we'll have sinned
If, in the lairig bothy, we do not fear the wind.

HAMISH BROWN

THE LAIRIG

Fin God made Buchan flat and gweed,
He'd nowt and corn in His heid.

And fin He gart yon Hielan's growe,
He'd hielan' ongauns in His pow.

But fin He laid the Lairig doon,
Dyod, fa kens fut wis in His croon!

J. C. MILNE

SGORAN DHU

Images of beauty and of destruction:
The pool, black as peat, still as a blade.
No man so strong of limb but its current is stronger.

The tarn, luminous verdigris, still as a jewel.
No sound save, once, a thunder of snow from the corrie.
No man so hot of blood but finds death in its water.

Summit of Sgoran Dhu, snow driving dim on the blast.
Far below, Loch Einich, precipice-sided and sombre.
No man so sure of self but here he must tremble.

Here man escapes from the futile sense of safety,
The busy and cheerful acts that invade the soul.
Here the Destroying Angel smites and they fail.

And he knows again the sharpness of life, its balance,
The mind springing and strong poised against danger and pain.
Nothing avails him here but the mind's own fineness.

NAN SHEPHERD

CAIRNGORM, NOVEMBER 1971

The mountain where I danced on moonlit stones
Has killed children.
Itching with cars, stitched with lifts,
Scabious with litter,
Forced to swallow human waste,
Provoked beyond millenia of patience
It killed.
And these were children.
They were not those who, sensing
The mute hostility of mountains,
Serve slow apprenticeship and by respect
Gain grudging tolerance.
Children:
Who rightly saw through gain and goods
And tried for deeper meaning.
Did they too readily accept
The World's urging to 'Have it Now'—
Bane of peace, frustrator, demon—
And try too hard?

So Ferlas Mhor looms by the cairn
And waits and watches.
Others will come. We make it so.

MARTYN BERRY

BEYOND FEITH BUIDHE

Six children, dear God, died out in this waste.
Six, children, laughing, crying,
Who came in morning innocence; trying
Of life to make haste.

White miles that cannot let us be
And blue skies of tempting power;
All life finds finality; somewhere, its hour
Of peace—and yet, remains, for us, all mystery.

The thousands have passed this way before
And thousands will come again;
Like spindrift flinging, in great joy or pain
Pass on and come no more.

HAMISH BROWN

ROTHIEMURCHUS

Gyang ower by Rothiemurchus whan the snaw lies thick
  And the cauld air glowing;
Gyang ower by derk Loch Morlich whan the wind growes quick
  Wi snell, snell blowing.

Pit smeddum in yir hairt wi frostit lungs straining
  At the lang tchyauve climbing
Neist the black ice-yokit lochan wi yir strength waning
  And the eye-sweit blinding.

Hear the steady drips slowing in the freshing drift
  In the gaithrin mirk
As the shargar sun faas early fae the efternin lift
  And the wind like a dirk.

See the stane-grey clouds that lower ayont the hills
  As the gale strengthens;
Syne the cauldrife air growes derker and frichtsomely chills
  Till yir stride lengthens.

It's the first feather flakes that are dauncing ower the moors
  In ghaistly birl;
It's the murdering Cairngorm blizzard that swiftly smoors
  Neth its deidly swirl.

There's a log hut faintly looming its grey wraith form
  And the lamp lowe's gleam;
There's werm air tae lave you and bield fae the storm
  Wi its cheated scream.

COLIN LAMONT

THE SPIRIT OF THE CAIRNGORMS

It is good to see the sunshine ebb on distant hills
and the dark shadows of the night rise from the valleys.
It is good to hear an untamed stream roar and lap through
empty wildernesses where nothing human meets the eye
and stunted trees sway dimly in the gusts of driving rain.
It is good to watch the creatures of the wild move freely
amid the moss and heather of the North. Bleak and stern
may be the scene, but in its rich meaning it has more to
tell than comlier views of southern climes.

You can sit and hear the ages whisper in the grass—
of honest joy, unsugared by pretence, unhampered by
    convention,
and yet unostentatious and quiet; of simple kindness that
gives without thinking of reward and does not feel exhausted
by its own benefaction; of sorrow that like wind needs
no expression to be understood; of courage unconscious
of glamour and applause; of life and death conceived to be
only two phases of one.

There is no haste, no frenzy in the majestic flow of days,
and solitude re-echoes the tread of passing time in terms
of shade and colour, without apprehension or regret.

AXEL FIRSOFF

AVIEMORE

The hills are stark, their outlines hard with frost.
From here, serene, inviolate; but closer, their ancient crusts
Erode into man-made scars, snow-filled and teeming.
The eagle eye pans in, and fixes on
A small irritation, a motion of molecules—
Skiers, swooping like disorientated rooks, go
Orderly like ants, pursuing
Relentless tracks up by twos, down in hordes—
Anthills are huge, snow slopes vast shouting spaces
Telescoped into silence. All that
Minute scurrying toil might make Sisyphus groan,
But from the geological viewpoint
They're just scratching the surface.
Makes a break, too (for us
Not Sisyphus).

JANET WALLER

STOPPING BY SHADOWS

High up, birches have a homely aspect,
small, like things we discover and recognise,
returning after an absence of many years.
Closer, they're almost transparent in the snow
and above, boulders big as cathedrals poise
—on the edge since pre-history.

Midday. I stop at the edge of the shadow
that has filled this space all winter,
the sun a white breath at the cliff-top,
a brief flame in the ice of a remote tree.
I turn and watch my own shadow dissolving
slowly in the luminous dark air

then take a cold step back to life,
skis hiss-hiss on snow-crystals
that spent all night quietly hardening.
Across the valley red and yellow figures
on a brilliant field jump into focus
like true events under a microscope.

ROBIN FULTON

FAR IN THE WEST

Far, far in the West
Is peace profound.
Clouds pillow the hill's crest,
Seas suck at the shore's breast
With rhythmic sound.

Faint, faint is the gleam
On ocean cast.
Dim, fantastic islands seem
Scattered fancies of a dream
When night is past.

Low, low is the thatch
Where peat smoke curled.
Children hurried to lift the latch,
Eager holiday gifts to snatch
From a bright world.

Lost, lost is that joy,
Utterly gone.
Years inexorably destroy
The unheeding happiness of a boy
At magic dawn.

Still, still there remain
Solace and balm.
The pure wind and the soft rain
Transmute the burden of care and pain
To blessed calm.

Far, far in the West
Is peace profound.
Clouds pillow the hill's crest,
Seas suck at the shore's breast
With rhythmic sound.

DOUGLAS FRASER

THEME AND VARIATIONS

Give me my scallop shell of quiet: let me go
Over the benty ground and high over the fells,
And further to the west, among the granite wells,
To hear the very streams of Iorsa where they flow:

Or over to Kintyre and Knapdale, and to know
The burning heather again, and all the former spells,
The golden plover's tune, and what the curlew tells;
And, rounding ancient hills, the white bird of the snow.

A highway and a way, they are not hard to win;
The fond wayfaring man, he shall not err therein;
They take you through the woods, above the fallow lea:

For past the red bracken, you find a rocky stair,
And so come out at last on the world open there,
Ridges white to the north, and islands in the sea.

W. P. KER

NETTLES

O sad for me Glen Aora,
   Where I have friends no more,
For lowly lie the rafters,
   And the lintels of the door.
The friends are all departed,
   The hearth-stone's black and cold,
And sturdy grows the nettle
   On the place beloved of old.

O! black might be that ruin
   Where my fathers dwelt so long,
And nothing hide the shame of it,
   The ugliness and wrong;
The cabar and the corner stone
   Might bleach in wind and rains,
But for the gentle nettle
   That took such a courtier's pains.

Here's one who has no quarrel
  With the nettle thick and tall,
That hides the cheerless hearthstone
  And screens the humble wall,
That clusters on the footpath
  Where the children used to play,
And guards a household's sepulchre
  From all who come the way.

There's deer upon the mountain,
  There's sheep along the glen,
The forests hum with feather,
  But where are now the men?
Here's but my mother's garden
  Where soft the footsteps fall,
My folk are quite forgotten,
  But the nettle's over all.

NEIL MUNRO

THE SHEILING

It stands alone
Up in a land of stone
All worn like ancient stairs,
A land of rocks and trees
Nourished on wind and stone.

And all within
Long delicate has been;
By arts and kindliness
Coloured, sweetened, and warmed
For many years has been.

Safe resting there
Men hear in the travelling air
But music, pictures see
In the same daily land
Painted by the wild air.

One maker's mind
Made both, and the house is kind
To the land that gave it peace,
And the stone has taken the house
To its cold heart and is kind.

EDWARD THOMAS

GLEN ROSA

Here time unfastens knot and strap.
The ages vanish: race, satrap
Erased from ethnologic map.

The wooden plough, the motor car
Are passing motes. These granites are
Perdurable with earth's royal star.

The five-fold streams descend and join
For one swift dash. The waters coin
Tormentil, speedwell and sainfoin

From sun-kissed banks. The mosses know
The prodding horns of stags. The slow
Rough buzzard creaks. Cloud shadows flow.

Retreat not, flesh. What though you feel
A worm beneath the falling wheel
As Rosa's mountains roar and reel?

From vertigo outspan and stand
Firm-placed as granite; eye and hand
Be soldiers under mind's command.

Doubtless your beat of pulse is frail,
Your grip of space a cloudlet's trail,
Your lease of time a falling sail:

But mind, determined from its birth,
Mandates you with the varied earth.
You drive the tiller o'er death's firth

Courageously, unknowing still
Mind's aim or what bright beings fill
The corries of the heart and will.

WILLIAM JEFFREY

A PICTURE

Broom pods crackling in the heat,
  Sweet faint scent of wild thyme and of grass,
Moving, illusive shadows on the bents,
  When the white gulls pass.

Blue sky and filmy clouds above,
  Uneasy waters fretting on the sand;
A far-off ship—a trailing plume of smoke,
  And a waiting, silent land.

Hills in a distant mantling haze;
  Sea-pinks and crowsfoot clothe the bank with grace,
An aspen, quivering there beside the burn,
  And perfect peace.

                    D. C. CUTHBERTSON

THE PAPS OF JURA

Before I crossed the sound
  I saw how from the sea
These breasts rise soft and round,
  Not two but three;

Now, climbing, I clasp rocks
  Storm-shattered and sharp-edged,
Grey ptarmigan their flocks,
  With starved moss wedged;

And mist like hair hangs over
  One barren breast and me,
Who climb, a desperate lover,
  With hand and knee.

                ANDREW YOUNG

ISLAND OF MULL

Island of Mull, island of joy:
wave-washed,
sun-topped,
wind-warmed,
peak-blasted,
with glens tight with hazel and oak,
straths grass-tawny, stepping waterfalls,
and mighty Ben More of the eagles
set high over all.

Island of Mull, island of joy:
dream-held,
burn-foamed,
deer-scattered,
gled-soaring,
with such the exile wears his memories.
As life's wrack ebbs his brief mortality
he still sees the green-richness of Ben More
rooted in the seas.

ANON
From the Gaelic of Dugald Macphail

THERE ARE GODS

There are gods in this place,
invisibly visible,
like eternity brooding
on the mountains of distant Mull—
the tears of time trickling inexorably
down their inaccessible faces,
leaving scars more unsightly than those
on a woman's body after child-birth.
This tiny runic temple speaks
of dead languages.
Voices come crying above
the creak of long-boats,
whilst out of the shimmering horizon
into the ebb tide of civilisation,
a leaf falls from a gorse bush
and is carried away to evolutionary obscurity.

Iona—Iona—the whisper is intense
above the vortex of thundering silence.

There are gods in this place,
they murmur in the sparse grass, the rocks,
and enrich the earth like the dung.
They soar aloft with the dour cry of sea birds
winging the black shore in search of sanctuary,
yet there is no sanctuary here
for gods—they cast no shadows,
have no forked tongues like mortals—
here on Iona.

C. L. RILEY

THE ISLAND OF RHUM

I stand on the deck of a small boat as rain sends bright daggers,
    splitting the dark waters of the sound of Eigg.
Before me towers Rhum. The mighty isle. The unalterable.

Old things I can understand. Nut brown of antiques. Curve of fine
    glazed ceramics. The Gothic arch, amphitheatres and columns,
    and all the marvellous works of ancient man.
But you, great isle, I can never truly know.

Your dark peaks run the depth of the spectrum, your cape of
    clouds throws light and shade in mystic scenes across the
    restless sea.

Timeless your story is,
    from lovely shores, through wooded glens deep ferned,
    upward to wild moors and rocky fastnesses;
    climbing where clouds pattern each dark buttress,
    where raven and eagle defy the fury of the winds that sweep
    in from the sea.

You, great isle, are truly venerable, the form of all things that are
    lovely and lasting. You are the architecture absolute. Sun and
    rain have drawn your tall columns, your deep corries hold
    vari-coloured cloud.
The rainbow builds your arches from peak to peak.

Your story is there in wild sweet sounds.
Thunder shakes the floor of your wide valleys where the stag
   bellows his love. The seal mourns on the shining rock and the
   sea pours its voices into shells that whisper along your bays.

Your story has no end, yet I will read each coloured word, and
   bright page as you rise in majesty each day from the dark
   waters;
as dawn gleams eternally from your tall mountains and your
   rocks throw back the pounding sea.

ROY FERGUSON

NIGHTMARE ON RHUM

The mountains are dragons
         battles of breathing beasts
                  ant armies
rising up to consume rash flesh
in contact with rock,
to fling me from the crest
so I float off
         over the Minch
                  into a green flash
for my last sunset.

At Kinloch first-sun comes sycamore-green
and the prim eiders call their own shock
at my dreams.
         I scrabble out from the tent to look
for comfort on the Cuillin spires

—but Askival is smothered in clag!

Was it a dream?
      was it a dream?
Or have the mountains eaten me?

JAMES MACMILLAN

110

THE ANCIENT SPEECH

(from *Eileann Chanaidh*)

A Gaelic bard they praise who in fourteen adjectives
Named the one indivisible soul of his glen;
For what are the bens and the glens but manifold qualities,
Immeasurable complexities of soul?
What are these isles but a song sung by island voices?
The herdsman sings ancestral memories
And the song makes the singer wise,
But only while he sings
Songs that were old when the old themselves were young,
Songs of these hills only, and of no isles but these.
For other hills and isles this language has no words.

The mountains are like manna, for one day given,
To each his own:
Strangers have crossed the sound, but not the sound of the dark
  oarsmen
Or the golden-haired sons of kings,
Strangers whose thought is not formed to the cadence of waves,
Rhythm of the sickle, oar and milking-pail,
Whose words make loved things strange and small,
Emptied of all that made them heart-felt or bright.

Our words keep no faith with the soul of the world.

KATHLEEN RAINE

GLEN PEAN

Glen Pean is in bright sunshine
As I lie by the lochan.
The sadness is nobody ever lives here now,
Just the birds, the insects, and the fish,
And the water moves and sounds too.

Still, save the water and the sounds breaking the great still
In the bowl of the valley, hot in the bright clear sunlight;
The faint metallic hum of the whirring wings of myriads of tiny
    insects,
The chew-chew-chew of the stonechat,
The splash of a fish breaking the surface of the water,
The lap of the waters on the rocks,
And the lambs off on the flanks of the valley.
They all share the sunlight with me,
The bright warm sun
With the breeze from the east,
And the hill opposite, with its scars and lumps and green,
And the vee at the end of the valley to the world beyond,
Enclosing us, cutting us from them perennially.

DENIS RIXSON

HILL LOVE

We looked over the white sea
after we'd climbed the brae
Back o Keppoch.
The isles were there as always:
abstract shapes abreast the tide
and phallic peaks in Skye.
We looked below us, down
the pulsing autumn slopes
gripped in a randy sun.
A stag roared and roared
and with his harem circled our knock
oblivious of all but lust.
We forgot the abstracts, the hills, the view . . .
in the bracken, by starlight,
had found our peace.

JAMES MACMILLAN

THE ROAD MOVES ON
(from *Kinloch*)

The road moves on, melting
To churned, barred wheel tracks,
Ephemeral chevrons in clay
That descend and ascend
To the horizon.
Across the Sound
Rise the Mountains, half hidden
In wavering mists.

It is the land of Beinn Sgritheal,
Beinn nan Caorach, and Beinn a'Chapaill,
The land of Druim Fada
And Beinn na Caillich.
Barren, aged
They lean, grey with hunger
For the bright, living waters
Of Loch Hourn.

Their challenge comes
As they lift into air.
It comes in great crescendos,
Disturbing mind and body
Like a Bartok concerto.
The mist swirls
And we feel the surge of effort
To recognise our need.

We sound a brave alarm.
Our battle cry,
Age to profound age
Reverberates.
We fight with tenacity,
Standing within the relentless stone,
Taking the savage instruction of the rocks
In physical pain.

Immersed in the conflict
That overwhelms us
We stand, staring at the sea.
We have not moved.
We turn back to the descent,
Holding our vision
And the defence of our estate,
We have reached a liberation.

DOROTHY NASH

LEAC A'CHLARSAIR

The air was vibrant round the hills,
As if a myriad strings
Moved varied wave beats,
Merging and rebounding,
Sounding,
Across the piles of peats,
The tones and overtones the sea flings
In broken chords on shelves and sills,
Far distant, far below
That field where moorland flowers grow,
And faint remembrance of sweet music stirred
By Leac a' Chlarsair.

Time to forget had filled my days
With crowded sense and thought,
Till, in the hour of ceilidh,
Suddenly chords were ringing,
Singing
Sweetly, passionately, gaily,
In cadence and theme so finely you caught
The rapture, the love, the pity, the praise.
Once more they overflow
That field where moorland flowers grow,
And living presence of sweet music stirs
By Leac a' Chlarsair.

LUCY TAYLOR

THE COOLIN RIDGE

Although you move among them as a friend
these mountains cannot take you for a brother:
you cannot imitate or comprehend
the loyalty they bear to one another:

but there are clouds, are clouds beyond all number
whenever the blue Atlantic brings them forth;
they gather at the sunset like a slumber
or fall like fear from the destroying North;

114

and there were men who came in summer there
upon the broken ridge, who stood intent
as carven marble, men who turned their eyes on

peak after peak, and through the cloudless air
beheld the Hebrides on the horizon;
and went away, and left no monument.

WILLIAM BELL

THE WITCH
(from *Skye*)

But for a breathing-space the witch,
Shedding her cloak of mystery,
Unveils her beauty to the light
Beyond the cold green glancing sea—
A moment, and then busily
Spinning, she swathes herself again
In a fresh web of mist and rain.

WILFRID GIBSON

SKYE
A skipper speaks

O a' the isles of this braid sea
That noo I navigate
There's nane that in the hert o me
Looms owre big wi' fate—
Exceptin Skye.
        Gliskin her crests
Infinite and serene:
Dochter of God, I cry, *sich breasts
Are nae for human een.*

JOHN GAWSWORTH

BECKON ME, YE CUILLINS

Beckon me, ye Cuillins?
Aye, beckon as ye may,
For I'm tired of all your whisperings
And tired of all your ways.
Ye seek to claim me as your own
And drench me with forgetfulness
Of other hills I've known.

Ye beckoned me, ye Cuillins,
I answered though I vow
I was but wandering hereabouts—
That's why I'm with ye now.

The Cuillin hills are beckoning
A slave, prone at their feet.
The Cuillin hills are reckoning
The mood in which to meet
The climber, gambler (whate'er he be)—
Unknowingly a slave,
Who'd seek their regal company
On ridge and cliff and cave.

A sunset with a golden gown
Bewitched another day
And drug of sleep the barrier
Twixt slave and Cuillins lay.

Why should I clothe in best attire?
The Cuillin hills did say,
Come mist! Come rain! Come thunderfire!
Come hail! And blast this day!

Beckon me, ye Cuillins? . . .
Aye, beckon as ye may,
I'll ne'er forget your golden gifts
In memory hid away—
When we made friends
With Wind and Rain
On a sunny summer's day.

K. G. P. HENDRIE

SKYE SUMMER

Skye rasps the mind. A tangle of harsh cries
is held among its sunny jagged rocks.
The roadways, lean as scraps of ill-spun thread,
wind up and over in a crazy pride
of twists and turns and sharp malevolence
of gradients, under a clanging sun
that shouts derision to the empty sky.

This is the adamantine core, the heart
of shrewish, graceless Scotland.

        Climb to the height;
withstand enduringly the very worst
of sunhard emptiness scooped like a skull
to sockets of black shadow. Very far
against the distance rise up like a dream
incredible in battlements the pure
miraculous Cuillin, and high above
the tiny gentle voices of the larks.

                ISLAY MURRAY DONALDSON

KINLOCH AINORT

A company of mountains, an upthrust of mountains
a great garth of growing mountains
a concourse of summits, of knolls, of hills
coming up with a fearsome roaring.

A rising of glens, of gloomy corries,
a lying down in the antlered bellowing;
a stretching of green nooks, of brook mazes,
prattling in the age-old mid-winter.

A cavalry of mountains, horse-riding summits,
a streaming headlong haste of foam,
a slipperiness of smooth flat rocks, small-bellied
  bare summits,
flat-rock snoring of high mountains.

                SORLEY MacLEAN

117

NO VOICE OF MAN

Ower the grey sentinel hills,
the cauld craig tap lours abeen
the dreepin weet blanket.
Fold of mist lyin, slippin
doon the braes tae
lochs an streams.
Wi a stealth befittin a dream.

The mochie dampness
settles on the gowden breem,
a leaf faas wi autumn's weight
a ripple on the water,
the heron glances, bodily stock still
upon a stane.

It wis niver aye sic a
bare nakit thing o beauty.
Beauty aye, but clad wonderfu
wi bonnie speakin folk.

A voice taen ower
by bleatin brutes.
A memory trampit on
by strangers,
wi laws and greed
impervious tae human
needs.

The misty vapour calms
the wid,
a minute dewdrap
springs on a newspun web.

A minute tear fulls an ee
swelling intae a sea
o emigrant ships stoked
wi misery.

RAYMOND FALCONER

SGURR NAN GILLEAN

(from *The Cuillin*)

But Sgurr nan Gillean the best Sgurr of them:
The blue-black gape-mouthed strong sgurr,
The sapling slender horned sgurr,
The forbidding great sgurr of danger,
The sgurr of Skye above the rest of them.

It would suit me, above every place,
To be on your high shoulder blades,
Striving with your rock greyest throat,
Wrestling with hard peaked surging breast.
In the ascent from the corrie
Foot on shelf, finger on little edge,
Chest to boulder, mouth to jutty,
On unbalanced step head undizzied,
Tough arm strong unturning
Till it grasps the sky-line of your fifth pinnacle,
Where will break on the struggle's head
The great dim sea of gabbro waves,
Knife-edge of high narrow ridges,
Belt of the dark steel surge.
An ocean whose welter is tight in rocks,
Its yawning mouths permanent in narrow chasms,
Its spouting ever-lasting in each turret,
Its swelling eternal in each sgurr.

I see the noble Island in its storm showers
As Mairi Mhor saw in her yearning,
And in the breaking of mist from the Garsven's head
creeping over desolate summits
There rises before me the plight of my kindred,
The woeful history of the lovely island.

Lochs of lochs in Coire Lagain
Were it not for the springs of Coire Mhadaidh,
the spring above all other springs
In the green and white Fair Corrie.
Multitude of springs and fewness of young men
To-day, yesterday and last night keeping me awake:
The miserable loss of our country's people,
Clearing of tenantry, exile, exploitation.

SORLEY MacLEAN

YE SIMPLE MEN

Now o'er the rugged Peasants' cot,
Once bright with Highland cheer,
A London brewer shoots the grouse,
A lordling stalks the deer.

What were your sins, ye simple men,
That banished from your home,
You left to deer your fathers' glen,
And ploughed the salt-sea foam?

Your fault was this, that you were poor,
And meekly took the wrong,
While Law, that still should help the weak,
Gave spurs to aid the strong.

JOHN STUART BLACKIE

A WARNING

If you are a delicate man,
And of wetting your skin are shy,
I'd have you know, before you go,
You had better not think of Skye.

ALEXANDER NICOLSON

DOING THE DUBHS

Said Maylard to Solly one day in Glen Brittle,
  All serious climbing, I vote, is a bore;
Just for once, I Dubh Beag you'll agree to do little,
  And, as less we can't do, let's go straight to Dubh Mor.

So now when they seek but a day's relaxation,
  With no thought in the world but of viewing the views,
And regarding the mountains in mute adoration,
  They call it not 'climbing,' but 'doing the Dubhs'.

ANON
(in *Scottish Mountaineering Club Guide*)

CORUISK

We lay upon the southern slope, and saw
The clear blue water lave the wrinkled stone,
And yonder lingered a thin white smoke,
Marking the feet of mighty Druim nan Ramh,
Upon whose battlements one ray of light
Shone like the fall of water in the air,
And all this imaged in the lake below;
Then, far above the meadow and the stream,
The seething cauldron of the coming storm,
Mysterious hollows filled with purple gloom,
'And wind-enchanted shapes of wandering mist,'
That half-enshrouded Ghreadaidh's solemn cliffs,
Or soared to Mhadaidh's many-headed crest;
High in the West the sombre-glowing eve,
And Bidein's turret struck with sunset fire.

W. C. SMITH

A'CHUILIONN

O far, fantastic line of notch and spire,
Strung dark across the yellow evening sky,
Mute, yet how eloquent of days gone by;
My heart is warmed by a forgotten fire.
For did we not, eager to satisfy
The zest of youth, set out with boot and rope,
And in our minds an ever present hope,
To find that magic place where eagles fly.
Garsven—the noble sweep from sea to crest,
The ridge beyond in sculptured lines expressed,
And every peak, each of resounding name;
These hills of early days now seem to say,
'Seek, nor abandon yet your quest, the way
Still upward goes—in content still the same.'

                                    A. G. HUTCHISON

FROM SKYE, EARLY AUTUMN

I hope that Death is a pass
Through the brown-green, blue-brown, blue-grey,
        grey ghost mountains,
With the mists hanging in the vales,
        hiding the hard places;
The calm sheep proving my path;
And the sun shining soft
On the loch I have left.

                                    M. L. MICHAL

THE MISTY ISLAND

From the lone shieling of the misty island
Mountains divide us, and the waste of seas—
Yet still the blood is strong, the heart is Highland,
And we in dreams behold the Hebrides.

                                    ANON

SOARING

Caught on the shoulder of Beinn Mhor on a slope
dropping so steeply away four feet below us
the island was only a bird's vision of
dunes and machair and heather slopes
eaten away with lochs and tarns
and the tapestry island
as fluid as wrack adrift on the open sea . . .

. . . we clutched at rocks, our mountain crowsnest
hovering unsupported, above
sheep on their green sky grazing, drifting
like clouds on a cloudless morning, the sky
retreating above us, about us, spinning away . . .

. . . as we talked ourselves to the top—
in flight from the depths
we rushed to the top, for the summit was real,
more real than the apparition of land
tempting us down . . .

You were walking ahead on a track
slightly below the ridge I was treading—
a raven suddenly shot from the cliff,
catching the sun on its back as it circled and rolled
hundreds of feet below me . . . I held onto stone
as my brain dipped, the mountain dissolved
and it seemed I was lying staring up,
up into the glen of the sky
where a raven was soaring upside down
under the river, the rocks, the heather . . .

                              CAL CLOTHIER

VIEW

I climb the Barra half-hill
and between my own dark summit and the other
in the evening light
the unexpected valley
in a green sea machair, narrowing
to where the grazing fails in iris.

Patchwork fields
are spread like childhood, and the man
who moves on them
from here seems child.

His haystacks are a brown dog's nipples;
dykes are scars around her body
with its thin and brindled, wind-bent hair.

The houses, roughly sown, are growing as they land,
not clustering, yet close enough;
their longer shadows meet.

I feel the valley drift away
in white-eye houses
and the insect sheep

and turning as the valley disappears,
and going down, I wonder why,
as the deer drift on another walk,
I take them as they seem
and make the unexpected fit
my eye. I think
from every half hill, looking down,
we make our pattern complete.

ROBIN MUNRO

OREADS

(Kyleakin, May 1969)

No, our kind cannot live with these
Solitudes, desolations, steeps and distances;
Mere emptiness to us the great spaces, where at ease
Mountains repose; they make nothing of us.
Their being is not of our mode or scale.

Some see a man's face on a crag, but it is not so;
Yet rock has a face that we see sometimes smile
And sometimes close. Five Sisters of Kintail—
But no kindred of ours
Those sisters of wind and gale.

Veering beneath crests of snow
Only wings know
The wind and know its flow; eagle and crow
In air unbounded come and go.
Like ant on lichened stone the dun stag pastures on the moor
   below.

But shepherd under hill in hovel of stone
Living companionable with crag and storm
May hear them speak, the alone to the alone,
Beyond the compass of the known.
Pipe music has the sound of distance in its drone.

Or a child may stray
Away on the wind hills as far as eye can see
Whose sight unhindered runs where summit meets the sky.
In the lens of a buzzard's eye the hills lie.

So lost,
Into how vast a loneliness we are gathered,
Into a strangeness how remote,
Existence without end; presences that yet
Protect us from invading night
And the unbroken silence of the dead.

KATHLEEN RAINE

THE DAM, GLEN GARRY

Ill-advised, in these parts, to shout
Suddenly out loud, or to invite
Responses in yourself you are not sure of.
In this romantic light.

Some would have been abandoned
To over-flowing passion.
Now, by the dam, the workers do
Their several jobs: or stop to smoke

A fag, to laugh, to talk;
And some with pleasure see
The hill; then, eyes descending
It is gone. Just so for me.

It is not numinous, but remains
A hill, a waterfall, a range.
Better to leave it so—and to escape
Whatever in the landscape may be strange.

ROBERT SYMMONS

APRIL, GLENGARRY

Winter kept us in the valleys
with still white woods, blue smoke through trees
and the ring of axes. We did not see the hill again
till the first days of another year,
the first winds from the West. Then ewes were lambing in
  green fanks
clean after snow, and the sun blinked once
in river Birches, brightly, as we climbed.

It was like a pilgrimage. The hill air flowed
like a clear and potent snowmelt, ruffling the cobalt blue
of sky and high tarn, tanning our eyes. We bathed in it,
as if come to the end of some ritual path
from a year of uncleanliness to this.
We felt restored. And returning, heard
almost with reverence the scattering
of Curlew-calls like raindrops from the source of Spring.

PHILIP COXON

126

THE FALLS OF GLOMACH

Rain drifts forever in this place
Tossed from the long white lace
The Falls trail on the black rocks below,
And golden-rod and rose-root shake
In wind that they forever make;
So though they wear their own rainbow
It's not in hope, but just for show,
For rain and wind together
Here through the summer make a chill wet weather.

ANDREW YOUNG

WESTER ROSS

from *Three Poems* (for the Highlands & Islands Advisory Panel)

Stone and rock,
Boulder and pebble,
Water and stone,
Heather and stone,
Heather and water
And the bog cotton that is not for weaving.

Peats uncut
And the orange moss
Under sharp rush
And spiked deer-grass,
Under tough myrtle
And thin blue milkwort,
And ever, ever,
The silver shining
Of the bog cotton that is not flowers.

The stones drop
From the height of the bens,
In the low houses
Of the dead crofters
The rafters drop,
And the turf roof:
Stone after stone
The walls are dropping,
And the bog creeps nearer
With the bog cotton for the fairies' flag.

NAOMI MITCHISON

THE THINGS OF THE NORTH

Let us give thanks for the things of the north . . .
    For blue, distant mountains tipping the curving brown sweep of
      moorland,
    for grey, drystane walls climbing the green shoulder of a sunlit
      hill,
    for hardy white houses, low-slung against the winds as if they
      had taken root,
    for scattered clinging woods and storm-bent trees telling of
      strength and solitude.

Let us give thanks for the things of the north . . .
    For dusty roads running to quiet farms deep in the glens,
    for lichened stones and hidden lochs placid beneath the cliffs,
    for amber burns that wend a gentle way through white
      bog-cotton,
    for all the silences that so delight and the clean scents of a
      Highland night.

Let us give thanks for the things of the north . . .
    For winds and rain that scour endless miles of rippling heather,
    for an elemental wildness that knows little of cities and towns,
    for an understanding that in stark harshness blinding beauty
      there abounds
    for those who walk and seek and find.

Let us give thanks for the things of the north.

RENNIE McOWAN

CLIMB IN TORRIDON
(Liathach, 1947)

Black, crumbling rock. Dead scree. The dolorous wind
that wails among the chimney-pots of hell.
Cloud smoking out of corries. Crooked teeth
set loosely in the wizened gums of Earth.
Slow-fingered shadows stroking furrowed hills.
Cold quartzite capped with diamonds by the sun.
The long ridge dropping perilously down
and down to dizzy dimness where a pool
catches the light among the pilèd grey
of crushing boulders dwarfed to grains of sand.

'We're climbing well today.
A team. No halts.
No lagging, sliding, fumbling for the map.
Only the click
of nails on rock—the quickened breath.
The lift, the straining muscle and the sweat.
The hammering of the heart. The expectant eye
leaping ahead to pinnacles of light.'
(The self-important ant upon a wall . . .?
The giant who spans a chasm in a stride . . .?)

A team. . . . Yet each of us, within himself,
Alone, as man forever is
alone on mountains. Silent with his thoughts.
Sad as the echoes. Happy as the streams.
Uncertain as the mist. Steady as rock.
And free as all the wandering winds that blow
across the ruined rooftops of the world.

BRENDA G. MACROW

LOCH LUICHART

Slioch and Sgurr Mor
Hang in the air in a white chastity
Of cloud and February snow
That less to earth they seem to owe
Than to the pale blue cloud-drift or
The deep blue sky.

Though high and far they stand,
Their shadows over leagues of forest come,
Here, to a purer beauty thinned
In this true mirror, now the wind,
That held it with a shaking hand,
Droops still and dumb.

As I push from the shore
And drift (beneath that buzzard) I climb now
These silver hills for miles and miles,
Breaking hard rock to gentle smiles
With the slow motion of my prow
And dripping oar.

ANDREW YOUNG

WHAT FINER HILLS?

Man-muckle was I or I saw
The mountains in their majestie
Unfauld afore my very een
Alang the length o Loch Maree.

Dark-green the pines on Islé Maree,
The larricks in a lichter green;
Grey-gowd, the brairdin twigs o birks
Added their beautie to the scene.

Blue were the waters o the loch,
Blue the Minch ayont Loch Ewe,
And still mair blue the lift abune
Whar Slioch raised his snaw-white broo.

Slioch, Beinn Lair, Beinn Airidh Charr,
Baosbheinn, Beinn Dearg, Beinn an Eoin,
The monie ridges o Beinn Eighe—
What finer hills are there nor thon?

Nae man that's wordy o the name
Could stand unmoved at sic a shaw
Or fail to satisfy the urge
To hansel their untrodden snaw.

J. K. ANNAND

DUNDONNEL MOUNTAINS

Through mist that sets the hills on fire
And rising, never rises higher
Looms a stone figure, gross and squat,
An idol carved out by the weather,
Face, limbs and body lumped together;
And while for none but mountain fox
Eagle or buzzard or wild cat
Its worship may be orthodox,
Death fawning on me from these rocks,
A false step would suffice
To make me both its priest and sacrifice.

ANDREW YOUNG

HIGHLAND REGION

It started with her shape on the map.
That elegant scatter of long-fingered islands,
Those westward indentations, capes, kyles
And spidery inlets laving
The roots of mountains, spoke to my child's mind
Of a miniature heraldic world:
Seas streaming like ponies' manes
But most unperilous, and needle peaks
No more forbidding than kitten's teeth.

Later I knew the dark truth of her:
The miles of bog weighing her down
Like sadness, or the memory of her dead;
Wind's pibroch in the soughing marram grass;
The Nessus' shirt of hopelessness
That history has burned into her back.
—And then I really loved her, as one loves
A woman for the lines around her eyes,
And she permitted it. And like a groom
Who hands down his mistress from her horse
I have been granted intimacies; but
One look into those sad and haughty eyes
Tells me she never can be truly mine.

VICTOR PRICE

ABOVE INVERKIRKAIG

I watch, across the loch
where seatrout are leaping,
Suilven and Cul Mor, my
mountains of mountains,
looming and pachydermatous in the thin light
of a clear half moon. Something swells
in my mind, in my self, as though
I were about to be enlarged,
to enclose informations and secrets
that lie just beyond me, that I would utter
in one short, stupendous sentence, to the everlasting
benefit of mankind and landscapes and me—
a pregnant feeling that is, naturally, caused
by love.

I know, half-moon-struck as I am,
the usual miscarriage will follow. I am beyond
the reach of miracles. And am glad of it,
thinking that, if this miracle were to happen
this time, it would be as if
Suilven should monstrously
move over to Cul Mor and after
coupling through human generations
drag himself back and sit
by his own lochside, indifferently
observing on the bogs of Assynt
a litter of tiny Suilvens, each one
the dead spit of his father.

NORMAN MacCAIG

MOMENT MUSICAL IN ASSYNT

A mountain is a sort of music: theme
And counter theme displaced in`air amongst
Their own variations.
Wagnerian Devil signed the Coigach score;
And God was Mozart when he wrote Cul Mor.

You climb a trio when you climb Cul Beag.
Stac Polly—there's a rondo in seven sharps,
Neat as a trivet.
And Quinag, rallentando in the haze,
Is one long tune extending phrase by phrase.

I listen with my eyes and see through that
Mellifluous din of shapes my masterpiece
Of masterpieces:
One sandstone chord that holds up time in space—
Sforzando Suilven reared on his ground base.

NORMAN MacCAIG

ASCENT

The white shape is Loch Fionn,
intimate with corners.
From here, the foothills of Suilven,
the white shape is Loch Fionn.

The green shape is Glencanisp,
detailed with rocks.
From here, the shoulder of Suilven,
the green shape is Glencanisp.

The blue shape is the seas
The blue shape is the skies.
From here, the summit of Suilven,
my net returns glittering.

DONALD G. SAUNDERS

HIGH UP ON SUILVEN

Gulfs of blue air, two lochs like spectacles,
A frog (this height) and Harris in the sky—
There are more reasons for hills
Than being steep and reaching only high.

Meeting the cliff face, the American wind
Stands up on end: chute going the wrong way.
Nine ravens play with it and
Go up and down its lift half the long day.

Reasons for them? The hill's one. . . . A web like this
Has a thread that goes beyond the possible;
The old spider outside space
Runs down it—and where's raven? Or where's hill?

NORMAN MacCAIG

NO ACCIDENT

Walking downhill from Suilven (a fine day, for once)
I twisted a knee. Two crippling miles to walk.
Leap became lower. Bag swung from a bowed neck.
Pedant of walking learned it like a dunce.

I didn't mind so much. Suilven's a place
That gives more than a basket of trout. It opens
The space it lives in and a heaven's revealed, in glimpses.
Grace is a crippling thing. You've to pay for grace.

The heaven's an odd one, shaped like cliff and scree
No less than they are: no picknicking place, but hiding
Forevers and everywheres in every thing—including
A two-mile walk, even, and a crippled knee.

You reach it by revelation. Good works can't place
Heaven in a dead hind and a falcon going
Or on the hard truth that, if only by being
First in a lower state, you've to pay for grace.

NORMAN MacCAIG

ASSYNT

High above Suilven an eagle soars
touching the sun with sinuous wings.
Below, in glens stained with the dark blood of history
sheep graze, and roe-deer browse, alert and nervous,
exploring the breeze, limbs poised for instant flight.
The eagle, argus-eyed, his victim spies,
with outstretched talons he plummets earthward,
a shrill cry, a feathered flurry—silence.
A cloud obscures the sun, then drifts on by,
a silent tribute, a minute's mourning,
and in a rockbound eyrie the king's children dine.
The wind transmits death's message,
and the birds listen, their voices stilled
for a brief moment, then, message received and understood,
erupt again—the quiet is broken.
Selfish, courageous, uncaring yet conscious of it all,
life, sweet savage life, goes on.

ALAN GILCHRIST

WHAT ARE YOU THINKING ABOUT?

We sit by the old tent,
With old scents and sounds
returning with the sun;
sucked from the earth,
watered by melting snow—
it's a dream of long ago.

An ant runs drunk on the groundsheet,
an owl shivers its voice on the afternoon,
a sheep bleats on and on (but distantly),
the river is all fishscales, the sun gold,
and Assynt stony white, and very old.

Through the smoke I see
A thousand sites and sigh
for the memories. I sigh
so audibly that she
asks a question.
I have to beg her
to repeat her words
for they sped, first swallows,
and passed me by
to star the sky.

JAMES MACMILLAN

PROSPECT OF A MOUNTAIN

Though cuckoos call across the kyle
And larks are dancing everywhere
To their thin bagpipe's air,
My thoughts are of the autumn day
I climbed that Quinaig, monstrous pile,
And striding up its slaggy brow
Stood outside time and space;
It looks so empty of me now,
More years than miles away,
The mountain-cairn might mark my burial-place.

ANDREW YOUNG

ON FOINAVEN

High up, I
see deer circle
in slow herds
the heel of Arcuil.

Higher, crows
eye me. I'm
prey too, picked-
out on stone, from time.

DONALD G. SAUNDERS

MARRY THE LASS?

Body black in the rock spine of Quinag
the thought intrudes: marry the lass?

Easy to spend a lifetime
with the minimum of fuss and sunny days . . .

He dismisses the thought, and the day
is spent struggling with unyielding rock.

Through evening the return is made,
fingers loose, grey eyes on the far Atlantic—

Also recalling her mother's ballooning outlines.
Home again. The piratical poet

Decides they will instead enjoy the
fashionable fruit of living in sin,

And muttering defiantly 'Many good years yet',
takes his boots off, has a dram, forgets the matter.

ANDREW GREIG

MARRIAGE ON A MOUNTAIN RIDGE

1
Like most, one way or another, ours
Has been through some dark couloirs.

I cannot swear to actual crevasses—
But have sensed them underfoot. (One night

On Beinn Fhada I lost my footing, and was fortunate
A rowan took my weight.)

This way I am better equipped
For keeping, if not to the spirit, the letter.

Crampons and pitons fitted, we face
The next assault, roped together. I also carry

An ice-axe—but fear to use it,
Lest it sink too deeply in.

2
Perhaps the hardest lesson
Is to accept the Brocken,

The Man with the Rainbow, as stemming
From myself; a projection

Of my own form. The cauldron
Below me, thin air.

In these rarefied labyrinths
The way forward

Is to focus
On a fixed point;

One hand gripping firmly
Its moral thread.

3
Whether scaling Etive
Of the shifting faces,

Or on the summit of Blaven,
Sheet-ice glistening

Through walls of mist,
It is all one. The tracks

We pursue are ours;
The zone we would enter

Not the mountain, but ourselves.
So for a moment, the mind

May afford to swing out
Over the wide abyss.

4
Then comes the point when body
And mind are one, each indefinable

Except in terms of the other.
Head and heart held

In a single noose. The Beast,
The Grey Man, cannot touch us here.

His footprints descending,
Identical with our own.

Later, victims of Time and Loss,
We will return and gaze there—

And marvel at such heights
Conquered, such blazing air.

                              STEWART CONN

THE STRATH OF KILDONAN

Skull stark,
These hills disturb us
With their silence.
Sheep stare from moonscape rocks
Rising above the tatters of the mist.
Half-submerged in bog,
A broken antler
Beckons.
Carious fences rot.
Wisps of cotton, like a dead man's beard,
Stir in the wind.
The lochan shivers.
Ill at ease among these alien gods,
We turn and hurry on
Towards Dounreay.

BETTY MORRIS

AT A RUINED CROFT
(Cnoc Bad a' Chrasgaith)

The walls are down to window height
    battlemented
In the wind the skelf of a lintel tilts
    like a balance

Just a piece of stick
In a year—or ten—one end will wear away
And it will fall
It's of no interest to anyone
There are no vandals
No one has bothered to derange it

The trees wave their besoms on the ridge
There is an echo of wind
The drills in the field are in corrugations

And at the east gable
A corroded pipe—one in a hill of 500 acres—
Works

JOHN MANSON

THE TALL SKY

The tall sky fallen in the sea
Lies drowning there.

Blue Morven riding on a horse of cloud
Cleaves bronze-bright air.

Whirlpools of the darksome moorland burn
Wave warrior hair.

And from Spring's choirstalls Amens clear and loud
End Winter's prayer.

ARTHUR BALL

MORE THAN PEOPLE
(from *A Cleared Land*)

More than people were cleared from these hills:
generations of feelings thin on the air
like a sharp wisp of bog-myrtle in autumn,
lumps of driftwood on a new-found shore
(fires for the first winter—nothing to save).

Then is diffused in *now*, as always.
Yesterday something was spilt and it lies
yet in acrid pools that'll never drain
till the forest that today is a forest of stumps
disturbs the air again with its thick breathing.

The roots are stiff and grey and catch your feet,
carved snakes of green lichen:
on them real snakes sun themselves.
Nevertheless the dead roots are fixed,
their hold on the thin soil is desperate.

Behind knuckles of rock, cotton-grass
survives with its wiry spine that bends in the wind,
survives to wave its ragged white flag.
Make this the emblem, for cloud-shadows
stumble vaguely across the moor like ghosts.

ROBIN FULTON

141

ABOVE BEN LOYAL

Above Ben Loyal one wandering cloud
Moves in a dream
From point to point of sky.
  No populace, no crowd,
Except the crowd of sunbeams silently
Walking within this meadow where I lie.

Broom, thistle, weave their shadows
  In this bright bed.
The sea is filled with glittering miracles
Between blue Hoy and Brindled Dunnet Head.

In Corsback, outposts of the dead
Feel the light imprint butterflies
Leave on their lonely mounds where green
Breaks into summer gold, and sighs.

Unseen,
The presences of other days
Rustle, and speak soft language in the wind.
The cloud, the sky, can see. We are the blind.

ARTHUR BALL

LION GATE

Above Stromness, the Hills of Hoy rise proud,
Like gardant lions; their heads concealed in cloud.

Above Stromness, the road curves inland; walk,
Leaving the shore where waves and sea-birds talk.

Walk inland, and the Hills of Hoy still loom,
Proudly defiant: 'Let the sky make room!'

Beside the Loch of Stenness, where rise proud
The Standing Stones, distance becomes a shroud

To veil the Hills of Hoy, yet still they seem
Like gardant lions, half-hidden in a dream

Of those who, before time, erected there
The Stones; skin-clad, their heads concealed by hair,

And strong eyes questing distances where crowd
Mist-shapes like unknown beasts half-hid in cloud.

VERA RICH

ROADS

The road to the burn
Is pails, gossip, gray linen.

The road to the shore
Is salt and tar.

We call the track to the peats
The kestrel road.

The road to the kirk
Is a road of silences.

Ploughmen's feet
Have beaten a road to the lamp and barrel.

And the road from the shop
Is loaves, sugar, paraffin, newspapers, gossip.

Tinkers and shepherds
Have the whole round hill for a road.

GEORGE MACKAY BROWN

SHETLAND, HILL DAWN

Even the sky is the colour of copper
hammered till it glows.

There are no black trees, there is no black
anything against the sky,
it is, still, an open land.

and hard behind the sun,
the colour of the ground turns malachite,
the copper in the rock, a thrill of green.

Before us, too, they found the hope
of islands, and the hope of dawns,
was of another day.

ROBIN MUNRO

RONAS HILL

Sullen Sullom Voe
visible
seen from the chambered cairn
on Ronas Hill.
There is always wind
always wind
Blowing in the mind
on Ronas Hill.
Are all summits hollow
man-empty
marking our beginning
marking our end?

HAMISH BROWN

A Certain Frivolity

THE LOST LEADER

(with apologies to the shade of Browning and to at least 73 others)

Just for a handful of summits he left us,
Just for a 'Dearg' to tick on his list.
Thus Munro's Tables have slowly bereft us,
Changed Ultramontane to Salvationist.
Raeburn was with us, Collie was of us,
Ling, Glover were for us—they watch from belays.
He alone breaks from the van and the freemen,
Climbs up his mountains the easiest ways.

We shall climb prospering—not thro' his presence,
Leads will inspirit us—not on his rope.
Deeds will be done while he boasts his collection,
Ben Vane to Braeriach, Mount Keen to Ben Hope.
Blot out his name then, record one lost soul more,
One more peak-bagger to collect them all.
Pelt him with pitons and crown him with crampons,
Leave him spreadeagled on Rubicon Wall!

DOUGLAS FRASER

147

THE OLD MUNRO BAGGER

'You are old Munro bagger,' the young man said,
'The locks that are left you are grey,
And yet you go on bagging tops all the time,
Now give me the reason I pray.'

'In the days of my youth,' Munro bagger replied,
'I remembered that youth would fly past,
And abused not my health and my vigour at first,
That I might go on right up to the last.'

'You are old Munro bagger,' the young man said,
'And pleasures with youth pass away,
And yet you lament not the hills that are done,
Now give me the reason I pray.'

'In the days of my youth,' Munro bagger replied,
'I remember that youth could not last,
So I saved up some hills that I could have done then,
To do them when life's nearly past.'

'You are old Munro bagger,' the young man cried,
'There are some you still have to do,
If death comes first, as you know that it might,
Whatever will come of the few?'

'I am cheerful young man.' Munro bagger replied,
'Some day you will understand too,
The challenge is not in the ones you have done,
But in those that you still have to do.'

'I am patient young man,' Munro bagger said,
'For I have enjoyed a long life through;
It is not the ones left that are keeping me going
But the new ones they are making me do.'

ANON
(First recorded in the Shenaval Bothy Book)

MOUNTAIN DAYS

I've had my share of mountain days in snow and rain and sun,
But not enough—for every day brought its own form of fun;
    Days lonely or gregarious,
    Grim days and days hilarious,
    Days of delights most various,
    I've sampled every one.

The day when, blind with stinging sleet, we stagger towards the
    height,
And boots are clogged, and bones are chilled, and fingers numb
    and white;
    A driving blast-and-blatter day,
    A set-the-teeth-a-chatter day,
    A mind-must-conquer-matter day;
    'Think of the bath to-night!'

The heather's dusty to the throat and weary to the feet;
The far too distant skyline is a-shimmer in the heat;
    A heavy, hot and hazy day,
    A climbing-would-be-crazy day;
    How cool the burn!—a lazy day
    To bathe and sleep and eat.

The day when the abysses yawn, the heart abandons hope,
With toes tense on a tiny hold while fumbling fingers grope;
    A where-he-goes-I-follow day,
    A does-my-laugh-ring-hollow? day,
    A 'Right-I'm-coming'-(swallow) day;
    Thank heaven for the rope!

The tingling frosty day whose dawn sets every top a-glow,
As up we hack through fastnesses of silent ice and snow.
    Then down—a sweeping, swooping day,
    A yodelling-and-whooping day,
    An almost loop-the-looping day,
    Glissading down we go.

Such days are shorter now and few (alas for heart and lung!)
My knees on screes are ill at ease; nor cling I where I clung.
    Yet even these bathetic days
    Recall the old athletic days,
    Those best and most poetic days
    When all the hills were young!

BARCLAY FRASER

THE LAST OF THE GRAND OLD MASTERS

As I strayed in the shade of the Buachaille
One cold and wintry day
I trod on a bod in a bog-hole
'Twas a climber old and grey.

'Now why do you lie 'neath the Buachaille?'
I asked that man of clay
With a curse and a mirthless chuckle
He to me these words did say:

'I'm the last of the Grand Old Masters
The Tigers of Yesterday
When the March of Progress passed us
We were left to Fade Away.

I was down with Joe Brown in Llanberis
When first he made his name;
With Brian, the Lion of Nevis
Set all Lochaber aflame.

Joe Brown lost his crown to another,
Though the legend lives on as before
And Brian the Lion is muzzled—
For him it's Lochaber, No More.

MacInnes has finished with pitons,
The Message won't ring any more;
Doug Haston has passed on his crampons
To Tiso's Alpine Store.

Now the Creag Dhu just make do with Moderates
Or maybe Curved Ridge in the Snow;
Jim Marshall's in partial retirement
And recording his hundredth Munro.

I've had ale by the pail in the Kingshouse
Tried anything once for a laugh
I've played with a maid at Glenbrittle
And gambled in Lagangarbh.

Now the beer's far too dear in the Kingshouse
There's no one will stand me "a half"
There's a shortage of maids in Glenbrittle
And the Police have closed down Lagangarbh.

Oh six stalwart climbers from Currie
Shall write me an epitaph drab
With a text from the works of Bill Murray
Writ in gold on a grey granite slab.

I'm the Last of the Grand Old Masters
But now I am old and grey
When the sweat on my neck turns to verglas
You will find I have passed away.'

On the pitiless slabs of the Nordwand
Where the bivouac sites are few
The Ghosts of the hosts of Old Masters
Are calling this warning to you:

Live it up, fill your cup, drown your sorrow
And sow your wild oats while ye may
For the toothless old tykes of tomorrow
Were the Tigers of Yesterday.

                              TOM PATEY
(*Tune:* 'Carnival of Venice' *or* 'My Hat, it has Three Corners')

MACINNES'S MOUNTAIN PATROL

Inspired by a Press cutting which quoted Hamish as saying: 'The time is not far distant when Dogs will replace Policemen as Mountain Rescuers.'

Dedicated to Scotland's leading philanthropist and his gallant pack of Avalanche Dogs.

Ghillies and shepherds are shouting Bravo
For Hamish MacInnes, the Pride of Glencoe
There'll be no mercy missions, no marathon slog
Just lift your receiver and ask them for DOG

Chorus: That four legged friend, that four legged friend
He'll never let you down
When the Heat is on, you have only to send
For that wonderful one two three four legged
friend.

Deceased on the piste, or deranged on the schist,
Maimed in the mountains, marooned in the mist,
Dead or dismembered, the victim is found
By Hamish MacInnes's Merciful Hound.

Chorus: That four legged friend, etc.

Occasional mischief is wrought by the dogs
On Englishmen, Irishmen, Welshmen and Wogs
Their only concern is to further the lot
Of the blue blooded true blooded patriot Scot.

Chorus: That four-legged friend, etc.

They come from their Kennels to answer the call
Cool, calm and courageous the Canine Patrol
Sniffing the boulders and scratching the snow
They've left their mark on each crag in the Coe.

Chorus: Those four legged friends, etc.

TOM PATEY

(*Tune: verse* 'Anthony Clarke'; *Chorus:* 'The Four Legged Friend', or
anything else that comes to mind)

WEATHER RHYMES

I   'If the mist comes down, just sit still'
Is the sage advice in the book;
But you'd eat your own skeleton
If the advice you took.

II   Weather's truth is most often hid
In murk and driving rain,
Yet still we head off north or west
And risk the hills again.

III   Hope is incomprehensible!
For, with sodden skin and blinded eye
And feet well mired from bog and brae,
This battered hope looks up, to cry:
'Tomorrow the rain will go away.'

IV   I dreamed of a great mountain
To be climbed next day
But the rain came down in torrents
And washed it all away.
I dreamed of a great exploit—
Headlines in the news!
But all we do is fester
And put on endless brews.

V   Too much wind is wearing
But too much rain is sad;
Better Ardnamurchan
Than Torridonian slab.
There you catch the breezes
And have a dribbly nose;
Better than the Gorms
That tend to freeze the toes.

VI   Morning warning:
Red sun,
Rains come.

HAMISH BROWN

TO A MIDGE

Wee strippit irritating beastie
Wha daurs o me to mak a feastie
An finds the juice o me sae tasty,
Ye can digest;
Ye needna crawl awa sae hasty
Ablow ma vest!

I hae a bottle here o lotion,
A sticky, smelly kind o potion,
That's guaranteed tae cause commotion
Tae midge or flee;
I'll sort ye fir yir wicked notion
O bitin me!

Curse on yir clan! I'm dune wi jokin;
For chreech ye dinna gie a docken;
So now a smokin fire I'm stokin
Wi breckans green—
Aye, deil! yons fairly got ye chokin,
An bleared yir een!

Let TOWERISTS seek from every nation
This land's romantic desolation;
Thou MIDGE will give them irritation
Beyond all ills:
At dusk they'll dance with desperation
On muirs and hills.

EILIDH NISBET

MOTIVE FOR MERCY

They sucked at the sweat on his forehead;
they rode on its beads through his hair,
and round the round dome of his baldness
they pate-hopped to copulate there.
They played first to sit on an eyelid—
'Beware of the slap of the hand!'
But rooting about in a nostril
was more than the fellow could stand.
He swished in the air rather vaguely,
not wishing, some say, to do harm;
and one too intent on its love-life
he caught in the cup of his palm.
Now—surely the essence of mercy?—
he mauled only maiming to try;
then flung it hard earthward abjuring,
'Learn wisdom re-learning to fly!'
He could have crushed dozens on dozens;
but Thomas the Doubter has said
there was damn all of mercy about it—
he wanted no blood on his head!

KEN MILBURN

AYE, THERE'S HILLS

Aye, there's hills, they say, rise tae the cloods
An peaks the likes o dreams, mun;
But gies the auld an weel-kent bens—
We'll kaik wirsels at hame, mun.

Aye, there's hills, they say, wi burns o ice
And unco things an a, mun;
Ye'd better bide wi tweedy braes—
Wir doucer hills o hame, mun.

Aye, there's hills, they say, tak affy time
Tae sclim richt tae the cairn, mun;
But whaur's the sense in that ava?—
I'll hae ma piece at hame, mun.

HAMISH BROWN

155

THE SCOTTISH MOUNTAINEERING CLUB SONG

Oh, the big ice axe, it hangs on the wall,
With the gaiters, and the gloves, and the rope, and all;
But we'll polish off the rust, and we'll knock out all the dust,
  When we go up to the mountains in the snow.
Then our raiment stout shall the cold keep out,
And the good old axe shall again cut tracks,
And the frozen slope shall call for the rope,
  When we go up to the mountains in the snow.

Chorus—Oh, my big hobnailers! Oh, my big hobnailers!
      How they speak of mountain peak,
      And lengthy stride o'er moorland wide!
      Oh, my big hobnailers! Oh, my big hobnailers!
      Memories raise of joyous days
      Upon the mountain side!

Then our cragsmen bold shall swarm up the shoots,
And shall win their way by unheard-of routes;
While others, never flagging, the tops and peaks are bagging,
  When we go up to the mountains in the snow.
Though the hailstones rattle, like the shot in battle,
And the whirlwind and blizzard freeze the marrow and the
  gizzard,
Though it thunder and it lighten, still our hearts it cannot
  frighten,
  When we go up to the mountains in the snow.

Chorus

For the best of the Club will then be afoot,
From the President down to the last recruit,
And a merry band you'll find us, as we leave the town behind us,
  When we go up to the mountains in the snow.
You may tell Tyndrum that we're going to come,
And at snug Dalmally shall our hillmen rally;
And a lot of other places shall behold our jolly faces,
  When we go up to the mountains in the snow.

Chorus

Let the Switzer boast of his Alpine host;
But the Scotsman kens of a thousand Bens—
Oh! their names are most supernal, but you'll find 'em in the
    Journal,
  As compiled by that enthusiast, Munro.
The Salvationist takes his pick from the list,
And the agile Ultramontane finds the exercise he's wantin'—
Each gets climbing that'll please him, as the mood may chance to
    seize him,
  When we go up to the mountains in the snow.

Chorus

Good comrades we, of the S.M.C.,
We're a jolly band of brothers, tho' we're sons of many mothers;
And trouble, strife, and worry—Gad! they quit us in a hurry
  When we go up to the mountains in the snow.
For our northern land offers sport so grand,
And in every kind of weather do we ply the good shoe-leather;
And from Caithness down to Arran, on the mountains big and
    barren,
You 'can trace our little footprints in the snow'.

Chorus

From the sunrise flush, when the hill-tops blush,
Till the moonbeams quiver on the ice-bound river,
We push attack and foray, over ridge and peak and corrie,
  When we go up to the mountains in the snow.
When the long day's done, and the vict'ry's won,
And the genial whisky toddy cheers the spirit, warms the body,
Then the ptarmigan and raven, far aloft above our haven,
  Hear our chorus faintly wafted o'er the snow.

Chorus

JOHN G. STOTT

THE BATTLE OF GLENTILT (1847)

A famous Duke tried to close Glen Tilt against a dour professor of botany.
The story is told by a medical professor.

O' cam' ye here to hear a lilt,
  Or ha'e a crack wi' me, man;
Or was ye at the Glen o' Tilt,
  An' did the shindy see, man?
I saw the shindy sair an' tough,
The flytin' there was loud and rough;
    The Duke cam' o'er
    Wi' gillies four,
    To mak' a stour,
    An' drive Balfour,
Frae 'yont the Hielan' hills, man.

The Sassenach chap they ca' Balfour,
  Wi' ither five or sax, man,
Frae 'yont the braes o' Mar cam' o'er,
  Wi' boxes on their backs, man.
Some thocht he was a chapman chiel,
Some thocht they cam' the deer to steal;
    But nae ane saw
    Them, after a'
    Do ocht ava'
    Against the law,
Amang the Hielan' hills, man.

Some folk'll tak' a heap o' fash
  For unco little end, man;
An' meikle time an' meikle cash
  For nocht ava' they'll spend, man.
Thae chaps had come a hunder' mile
For what was hardly worth their while;
    'Twas a' to poo
    Some gerse that grew
    On Ben Mac Dhu
    That ne'er a coo
Would care to pit her mouth till.

The gerse was poo't, the boxes fill't,
  An' syne the hail clamjamphrie,
Would tak' the road by Glen o' Tilt,
  Awa' to whar they cam' frae.
The Duke at this put up his birse,
He vowed, in English and in Erse,
    That Saxon fit
    Su'd never get
    A'e single bit
    Throughout his yet,
Amang the Hielan' hills, man.

Balfour he had a mind as weel
  As ony Duke could hae, man,
Quo' he, 'There's ne'er a kilted chiel
  Shall drive us back this day, man.
It's justice and it's public richt.
We'll pass Glen Tilt afore the nicht.
    For Dukes shall we
    Care a'e bawbee?
    The road's as free
    To you and me
As to his Grace himself, man.'

The Duke was at an unco loss
  To manage in a hurry,
Sae he sent roun' the fiery cross
  To ca' the clan o' Murray.
His men cam' down frae glen an' hill—
Four gillies and a writer chiel—
    In kilts and hose,
    A' to oppose
    Their Saxon foes,
    An' gi'e them blows,
An' drive them frae the hills, man.

The Sassenachs they cam' doon to Blair,
  And marched as bauld as brass, man;
The glen was closed when they got there,
  And out they couldna pass, man;
The Duke he glower'd in through the yet,
An' said that out they shouldna get;
    'Twas trespass clear
    Their comin' here,
    For they wad fear
    Awa' his deer,
Amang the Hielan' hills, man.

159

Balfour he said it was absurd;
   The Duke was in a rage, man;
He said he wadna hear a word,
   Although they spak' an age, man.
The mair they fleeched, the mair they spoke,
The mair the Duke blew out his smoke;
      He said (guid luck!)
      Balfour micht tak'
      An' carry back
      His Saxon pack
Ayont the Hielan' hills, man.

The gangin' back was easier said
   Than it was dune, by far, man;
The nearest place to rest their head
   Was up ayont Braemar, man.
'Twas best to seek Blair Athole Inn,
For they were drookit to the skin:
      Sae syne they a'
      Lap o'er a wa',
      An' ran awa',
      Wi' a guffaw,
An' left the Hielan' hills, man.

An' sae the battle ended then,
   Afore 'twas focht ava', man;
An' noo some ither chaps hae gaen
   An' ta'en the Duke to law, man.
Ochon! your Grace, my bonny man,
   An' ye had sense as ye hae lan'
      Ye'd been this hour
      Ayont the po'er
      O' lawyers dour,
      An' let Balfour
Gang through your Hielan' hills, man.

                    SIR DOUGLAS MACLAGAN

SOUTHWARD BOUND

As I came o'er the Devil's Stair
  The rain sent Etives down my spine,
A Clachlet weighed my shoulders down
  —And Kingshouse bar had closed at nine.

As I came o'er the Blackmount road
  Night's gully-walls closed in on me,
And in the dark my soul fared forth
  —On nine miles uncompacted scree.

As dawn came grey by Orchy-side
  My thoughts were stark peat-blackened roots,
And all Glencoe was in my heart
  —And most of Rannoch in my boots.

As I come o'er the mem'ry now
  A Brocken-glory rings its woes,
A Crianlarich *alpen-gluhen*
  Flushes the deathly facts with rose.

And so I'll start, next free weekend,
  With visions of a sunlit track,
Hope, Nevis-high, within my heart
  —And two skin-changes in my sack.

J. F. A. BURT

FEELS

Awa te the hulls, awa
Owre hedder and stanes and snaw!
For ilka God's feel
Twa's made by the Deil,
But the hulls mak feels o's a'!

J. C. MILNE

161

SISYPHUS

Bumpity doun in the corrie gaed whuddran the pitiless
   whun stane.
Sisyphus, pechan and sweitan, disjaskit, forfeuchan and
   broun'd-aff,
sat on the heather a hanlawhile, houpan the Boss didna
   spy him,
seean the terms of his contract includit nae mention of
   tea-breaks,
syne at the muckle big scunnersome boulder he trauchlit
   aince mair,
Ach, hou kenspeckle it was, that he ken'd ilka spreckle
   and blotch on't.
Heavan awa at its wecht, he manhaunnlit the bruitt up
   the brae-face,
takkan the easiest gait he had fand in a fudder of dour
   years,
hauddan awa frae the craigs had affrichtit him maist in
   his youth-heid,
feelan his years aa the same, he gaed cannily, tenty of
   slipped discs.
Eftir an hour and a quarter he warslit his wey to the
   brae's heid,
hystit his boulder richt up on the tap of the cairn—and it
   stude there!
streiket his length on the chuckie-stanes, houpan the Boss
   wadna spy him,

ROBERT GARIOCH

CANEDOLIA

(an off-concrete scotch fantasia)

oa! hoy! awe! ba! mey!

who saw?
rhu saw rum. garve saw smoo. nigg saw tain. lairg saw lagg.
rigg saw eigg. largs saw haggs. tongue saw luss. mull saw yell.
stoer saw strone. drem saw muck. gask saw noss. unst saw cults.
echt saw banff. weem saw wick. trool saw twatt.

how far?
from largo to lunga from joppa to skibo from ratho to shona from
ulva to minto from tinto to tolsta from soutra to marsco from
braco to barra from alva to stobo from fogo to fada from gigha to
gogo from kelso to stroma from hirta to spango.

what is it like there?
och it' freuchie, it's faifley, it's wamphray, it's frandy, it's sliddery.

what do you do?
we foindle and fungle, we bonkle and meigle and maxpoffle, we
scotstarvit, armit, wormit, and even whifflet. we play at
crossstobs, leuchars, gorbals, and finfan. we scavaig, and there's
aye a bit of tilquhilly. if it's wet, treshnish and mishnish.

what is the best of the country?
blinkbonny! airgold! thundergay!

and the worst?
scrishven, shiskine, scrabster, and snizort.

listen! what's that?
catacol and wauchope, never heed them.

tell us about last night
well, we had a wee ferintosh and we lay on the quiraing, it was
pure strontian!

but who was there?
petermoidart and craigenkenneth and cambusputtock and
ecclemuchty and corriehulish and balladolly and altnacanny and
clauchanvrechan and stronachlochan and auchenlachar and
tighnacrankie and tilliebruaich and killieharra and invervannach
and achnatudlem and machrishellach and inchtamurchan and
auchterfechan and kinlochculter and ardnawhallie and
invershuggle.

and what was the toast?
schiehallion! schiehallion! schiehallion!

EDWIN MORGAN

A Backward View from the Cairn

LEVAVI OCULOS

'I have been in the hills all day;
'I have not heard the news.'
No, but you heard instead
The mountain mosses singing at your tread,
And saw the views
Heart-lifting, of the shadows in the bay.
    Down, down and down below
    You looked to where men count the days;
    But here, where winter stays
    And sudden drops his cloak and turns to spring,
    Is no such thing.

Here is the open heaven, spinning and standing fast,
Held on the big tops' shoulders; here is height
Soaring beyond mortality; and air
That moves eternal there
Which but to taste, teaches delight
And heals time past.
    And here the spring-foot doe
    Treading across the moss comes curiously,
    Here the white hare sits watching from a ledge
    And there, the very edge
    Of magic, whistling liquidly,
    The golden, golden plover wheel and go.

And hark! What others come?
Wild swans, the soul of storm,
Beating their great vans in the sky
And from long golden throats
Sounding out haunting notes,
The trumpets of an older chivalry;
And, tilting in the wind, the eagles
    Not of Rome.

But to come down again,
To leave the holy ground and tread the earth,
In from the brightness of infinity,
Casting the lost glow of divinity
Back to distress and dearth,
Cramping beneath the burdens—
    God, the pain!

Cry, for we left our Paradise today;
But when we turn and load
Accustomed burdens, grieving, if we say
'None knows what we forego!'
Then One says, low,
   'I, too, joyfully trod my hills and came away,
   'And bore a Burden up a stony road.'

MARION CAMPBELL

ON THE HEIGHTS

Once more the miracle, still unexplained—
  Content and strength and thankfulness renewed,
As though the spirit its true realm attained
  Here in this sunlit, still, high solitude.

From past and future, our whole dream of time,
  I am by strange enlightenment set free;
This moment's all; I know the *Now* sublime,
  Eternal, as the great reality.

Sorrows and failures, disillusion, pain,
  Pleasures, successes, all that life has been,
As spectrum colours fuse to white again,
  Mingle, accepted, in a joy serene.

I shall descend from this illumined height,
  Find doubt and fear and trouble to bemoan,
Yet even in gloom may I remember light
  And trust the certainties that here I've known.

O God who made the hills, to all who seek
  Grant their uplifted moment, that they so
See the far vision, hear the silence speak,
  And, past philosophy's surmisings, know!

W. K. HOLMES

MOUNTAINEERING BUS

Do you remember that day of the roaring storm,
The ice-plastered ridge and our growing alarm,
When we sheltered behind our heavy packs,
And Jim lost a crampon and Matt an axe,
And we thought the battering would never end?

Do you remember that day?

Do you remember that night of the one-room crush
When the wheel broke loose from the back of the bus,
And the crofter's wife let us use the phone,
And thirty-four people crammed into her home,
And it rang with the sounds of a ceilidh?

Do you remember that night?

Do you remember those months throughout the year,
The early starts and the piles of gear,
The rain and the sun and the distant snow,
The songs and the jokes and the heart-felt glow
Of fulfilling days well spent?

Do you remember those months?

Do you remember Ronnie and that greasy crack
When Elspeth got stuck and scraped her back,
Munro-bagging Malcolm and bothy-mad Bill,
And the night when Freda was lost on the hill
And Danny fell into the burn?
Do you remember . . . do you remember?
Is the bus still running, is it still the same?

The climbers will change, the hills remain.

RENNIE McOWAN

HOW SMALL IS MAN

Why climb the mountains? I will tell you why,
  And, if my fancy jumps not with your whim,
What marvel? there is scope beneath the sky
  For things that creep, and fly, and walk, and swim.
I love the free breath of the broad-wing'd breeze,
  I love the eye's free sweep from craggy rim,
I love the free bird poised at lofty ease,
  And the free torrent's far-upsounding hymn;
I love to leave my littleness behind
  In the low vale where little cares are great,
And in the mighty map of things to find
  A sober measure of my scanty state,
Taught by the vastness of God's pictured plan
In the big world how small a thing is man!

JOHN STUART BLACKIE

WHAT CALLED ME TO THE HEIGHTS?

What called me to the heights?
    Was it the wind?
One of those finer airs
That play around the mountain tops,
    Over grey rocks
And lichen-covered stones,
Stirring the tufted grass
That grows upon the edge?

What called me to the heights?
    Was it the wish
To rise above the plain,
And climb by scar and spire and crag
To some outstanding peak,
    Where sight may range,
Past rocky ridge and crest
Far over hill and dale,
Down to the silver sea?

What calls me to the heights?
Is it a dream?
Or vision flashing clear
Seen through a parting in the clouds
That veil this present life?
A sudden view,
Far o'er the hills of time,
Of that which lies beyond
The range of mortal sight?

Who calls me to the heights?
Is it strong death?
God's messenger, who comes
To bear the soul to highest Heaven?
There on some pinnacle
To rest awhile,
And resting there behold
Across unmeasured space
The Majesty of God?

LAWRENCE PILKINGTON
One of the Pilkington brothers who made the first
ascent of the Innaccessible Pinnacle.

THE OLD MOUNTAINEER

Far off, far off, so faint against the sky
Stood like a phantom wedge of amethyst
A shape that any would have surely missed
Save one who knew that mountain as do I.
Across the severing miles I gazed and paid
Tribute of gratitude for old delight
And strength renewed so often on that height—
A place of pilgrimage whence came mine aid,
Now so far off—farther than miles can reach
For me at last, who bear with other men
The tyrannies of mortal time, that teach
I shall not make that pilgrimage again.
Oh may my spirit still by memory share
The high serenity that blessed me there!

W. K. HOLMES

THE PERFECT GARDEN

I found a garden of thyme and thrift
Three thousand feet up a hill,
And other colours were blended in
With more than a gardener's skill.

Like rubies scattered by fairy hands
The wee *silene* spread
Hither and there in the quartzite screes
Of its windswept alpine bed:

All these, and more, in riotous wealth
Against a turquoise sky—
In the changing, glinting, hilltop light
As the shadows of clouds sailed by.

And I thanked the Lord for His lovely hills,
And for this dear land of ours,
And for strength to climb, and for eyes to see
His perfect garden of flowers.

WINIFRED ROBERTSON
The wife of A. E. Robertson, first man to complete
the Munros, in 1901

ON THE HILL

Out frae the wüd the gowk cries still,
And the gled hings owre the cairn;
But there is nae hind abüne the hill;
Nae stag doun be the burn.

Yet when the hill in a haary drift
Glimmers ahint the grey
The deer will gether atween the lift
And the bare rigg o' the brae.

A hameless herd wha aince wud spy,
Doun in the carse-lands braw,
The banners o' Scotland flauchter by
And the buskit buglers blaw.

WILLIAM SOUTAR

TO ALAN

You led me to the hills,
Taught me to scale the crags in safety.
On your rope
I tasted joys purer and more intense
Than any since. The intimate touch
And contact with the rock,
The thrill of danger faced and overcome,
The sense of space, the keen, clean mountain air
And that supreme delight,
All joys rolled into one, the climb achieved,
Relaxed in comradeship above the world
With senses keyed to highest pitch,
Flooding the mind with the sheer bliss
Of being alive. No questions and no doubts.

Now you are dead
And I no longer light of limb.
There may be mountains yet for me
But less ambitious climbs
And pleasures more reflective and subdued.
Is our shared glory lost?
Will it be meaningless at last?

Nothing is lost, for I have come to think
That when I face the final challenge, death,
The sum of those enchanted days,
The wind, the clouds,
Mosses and pools and stones—
All that we heard, saw, felt,
Flashed on the screen of fading consciousness,
Will fuse together in a pattern
That is the meaning of life; and I may hear
(Who knows?) as in those happy, youthful days,
Your calm voice guiding and instructing me
Until I scale that final peak
And view
The unimagined vistas of eternity.

                                        DOUGLAS FRASER

THEN AND NOW

Many years back was an evening;
It is evening again.
I am both then and now—
Then, in the evening of moths
Sprung with the heather's dust
From the brushing feet;
Then, when there was only
Sea hush and wind hush
Sea scent and wind scent
Honeysuckle pale among rock
The Cuillin black on the sky—
Then was an evening.

It is evening again.
Now, in the evening of rain
I feel the fire's warmth
Less strong than the years' coldness.
Many years have passed
And now in the evening
There is rain.

In that evening
We climbed the Cuillin Ridge
Saw the moon rise and set
Saw the dawn grow;
We knew the roughness of the rock
The burning of the sun.
The day burned through us—

Many years have passed;
It is evening again.
Now in the evening
There is rain.

ANNE B. MURRAY

FOOTPRINTS

The bare soul will tramp
deep footprints over trackless snow
to feel less alone
in the dead hills'
emptiness.

Silly, for a night of wind and thaw
will wipe the saucer of spilled life.
Where we set blue footprints,
tomorrow, is grass.

HAMISH BROWN

AMONG HIGH HILLS

From year to year I shall return
To these high hills and look upon
Their agelessness: from them I learn
To shape a spirit out of stone.

The sea is restless and the sky
Is changeful as the erring day:
I know their fellowship and I
Would be less vagabond than they.

I have a fierce and human trust
That there is stay amid all strife,
And that the mind of man is thrust
Up from the turbulence of life.

Therefore, lest I lose hope, I'll turn
To these high hills and look upon
Their steadfastness: from them I learn
A living faith—From them alone.

WILLIAM SOUTAR

A WIND FROM THE WEST

To-day a wind from the West out over the hills
    came blowing—
  Ah, how it made dim dreams and memories
    start!
And I thought that I smelt in my room the wild thyme
    growing,
  And the scent of the sweet bog-myrtle filled my
    heart.

Go back, O breath of the hills! Would that we
    went together!
  Tell how their lost child fares.
Whisper among the bracken, and say to the broom
    and the heather
  That still my heart is theirs.

Steal quietly as a dream along the glens that we know:
  The glens that shall fade from me only when I
    lie dying;
Sink into peace in the quiet place silent and low
  Where the dust men know not is lying.

Say still my heart is theirs—
  Tell them I never forget,
That they never are drowned in my joys, nor crushed
    in my cares—
  That I love them yet.

Yet! Ah there's never a heart like them now,
  Nor ever can be again;
None, living or dying, like those dead hearts that are
    lying
  Away in the West in the rain!

LAUCHLAN MacLEAN WATT

ANTE MORTEM

I will attempt the Capel track
Old, stiff and retrograde
And get some pal to shove me on
Should resolution fade,
For I must see black Meikle Pap
Against a starry sky
And watch the dawn from Lochnagar
Once more before I die.

The golden plover whistled there
Before the Fall of Man
And you can hear the brittle croak
Of lonely ptarmigan,
No heather there but boulders bare
And quartz and granite grit
And ribs of snow, bleak, old and grey
As I remember it.

And if I do not make the top
Then sit me on a stone,
Some lichened rock among the screes
And leave me there alone,
Yes, leave me there alone to hear
Where spout and buttress are
The breeze that stirs the little loch
On silent Lochnagar.

SYD SCROGGIE

GROWING OLD

I shall be quite content,
    When the high tops are out of reach,
    To watch the young set out with axe and rope,
    Knowing the lessons that the hills can teach,
    Knowing their boundless scope,
    I shall be quite content.

I shall be quite content,
When all my feeble lays are sung,
To hear new voices raised in keener song,
To know the hills can still inspire the young,
The hardy, fit and strong.
Yes, I shall be content.

I shall be quite content,
    Knowing the mountains will endure
    To lure my children's children with their spell
    Something I found among them that is sure,
    Something that served me well,
    And I am quite content.

DOUGLAS FRASER

THE HILLMAN LOOKS BACK

What is it that stirs the heart and mind,
Quietly and insidiously biting deep
Until it is a part of self
And irremovably entwined
With other loves?

It is deeper than the young man's vigour,
Or the joyful crunch of speeding
boots in snow,
The swinging axe and the boasting tongue
Of excited youth.

The secret lies in many, quieter things,
Spanning the years, absorbing and enfolding
In the peaceful thrills,
Linking the mind with vanished races
And quiet and ancient hills.

Images jostle for the heart's possession,
The rolling moorland and wrinkled rocks,
Swirling mist and nervous deer, as the
Foaming burns make their gurgling way to
Black and hidden lochs.

Blue ramparts barred with snow,
Deep wooded glens, and the secret places
And the poignant traces of crumbled dwellings,
All these, sear and grasp, and the hillman knows

Their eternal clasp.

RENNIE McOWAN

WHEN I AM DEAD

When I am dead,
And this strange spark of life that in me lies
Is fled to join the great white core of life
That surely flames beyond eternities,
And all I ever thought of as myself
Is mouldering to dust and cold dead ash,
This pride of nerve and muscle—merest dross,
This joy of brain and eye and touch but trash,

Bury me not, I pray thee,
In the dark earth, where comes not any ray
Of light or warmth or ought that made life dear:
But take my whitened bones far, far away
Out of the hum and turmoil of the town,
Find me a wind-swept boulder for a bier,
And on it lay me down,
Where far beneath drops sheer the rocky ridge
Down to the gloomy valley, and the streams
Fall foaming white against black beetling rocks
Where the sun's kindly radiance seldom gleams:
Where some tall peak, defiant, steadfast, rocks
The passing gods: and all the ways of men
Forgotten.

So may I know
Even in that death that comes to everything
The swiftly silent swish of hurrying snow:
The lash of rain: the savage bellowing
Of stags: the bitter keen-knife-edge embrace
Of the rushing wind: and still the tremulous dawn
Will touch the eyeless sockets of my face:
And I shall see the sunset and anon
Shall know the velvet kindness of the night
And see the stars.

HUGH BARRIE

This poem appeared in the *Glasgow University Magazine* only some months
before the Hogmanay 1927 tragedy in the Cairngorms that cost the lives of
Barrie and Baird.

WHEN I DIE
(from *All Flesh is Grass*)

When I die
shelter me in the green
curve of a green hill where yet my blind
eyes may behold the lean
spears of the slanting rain.

And I may move again
with the great tides of cloud and wind
that cover me.

BRENDA G. MACROW

ONE THOUSAND FEET
OF SHADOW
(For Dave)

The whale got my friend,
The big whale hull down in Loch Linnhe,
The big white whale ghosting under a frore sky,
High snowfields windless, frozen shoulders sheer.
The Carn Dearg buttresses reared their shattered backbones,
Shadows skulked in the lee of the plateau.
My friend turned to see
His mate making a high step,
Their bodies light with relief
After the hours of tensed effort upwards.
He caught a spike in a lace,
Toppled, slid, plummeted off the edge,
Fell one thousand feet of shadow.
The corrie gaped its whale jaws,
The great gut constricted,
A cold draught came from the depths,
Stiffening rapidly the torn skin,
Coagulating blood, limbs out of true,
And my friend's face transfixed
In the tearing gasp of his last breath.

DAVID CRAIG

LOOKING DOWN A HILL

From here, boulders are pebbles,
the ground a painted map
and the route
invisible.

Bright tiny figures
sprawl at binocular speed
up some new route.

When they have added to this cairn
their stone, my sun
will have set coldly, over there.

No use shouting down help;
describing my route.
No use,
we make our mountains as we climb.

A. R. THOMPSON

MOUNTAIN CREED

The last thing, the very
Last thing, of which
I am afraid
Is death.

I have a wholesome
Respect for wit, gentleness
And even cunning, and the pain
That these things cause, but dying

I hold as nothing. Each and all
Go, and a show of bravery,
That famed upper-lip,
Is no proud boast.

Let a man be afraid
Of pain, certainly, but why
Should we delude oursevles that
Moving on is something great? Why?

Up in the mountains, on a face
Of sheer rock, with the winding
Rain sucking at my fingers
And a boot-nail holding,

Barely holding, mark you,
My body poised between this
And that below, I know fear, not
However, the fear of dying, but the fear,

Pure and simple, of falling, failing
To achieve the set purpose imposed
Upon myself by the mere existence
Of that high place.

The last thing, the very
Last thing, I am afraid, is death.

HUGH C. RAE

FAUR WID I DEE?

Faur wid I dee?
On a bed in the room o' a hoose i' the hert o' a toon?
Streekit oot straucht in a dark kist? Happit doon?
Grievin folk and grave stanes stan'in roon?
Na, nae for me!

For I wid dee
Awa up yonner on braid Beinn a' Bhuird or Ben A'an,
Faur there's scowth for the Lord te tak' yer spirit in han',
And a wind te blaw owre the bonnie bare banes o' a man,
Ay, there for me!

J. C. MILNE

TO THIS HILL AGAIN

I like to think one day
(if the world lasts)
I will come secretly
to this hill again.

It may take generations
(from dust to seed to bird)
before my littleness finds
in this loved place
the dream peace
that would satisfy
as immortality.

JAMES MACMILLAN

THE HILLS OF GOD

I wandered up an autumn loaning,
Leading to the hills of God;
And there I met a gold-bright maiden
Gathering brambles in the grass.

'O have you seen my dear blood-brother,
Eagle-eyed and lightning-footed?
We plighted troth in this green loaning:
He sought a star, and could not tarry;

'And thus I wed a dark-browed shepherd,
Older than he, and quiet-spoken;
Who waits for me to lay his table;
So fare you well, whate'er your journey.'

I came again to that grey loaning,
Leading to the hills of God;
But found no more the gold-bright maiden;
Seeded the fruit, the grass untrodden.

Split stones marked out a ruined cottage,
A twisted thorn crouched o'er its hearthstone;
By trackless waste, through fog and tempest,
Alone I seek the hills of God.

Where these have gone, now I would follow,
My little lamp of faith to guide me,
To prove no dream my lost blood-brother,
My gold-bright maid, her dark-browed shepherd,
Enfolded in the hills of God.

A. A. BUIST

POEM, 1972

We saw the Brochan spectre from
The crags of Ben-y-Glow,
We heard the Grey Man's footfalls crunch
In Sputan Dearg's snow,
And from the Monadh Liadhs saw
Criss-crossing in the sky
A thousand golden circles and
A thousand suns forbye.

We saw a blood-red cirrus sky
Which crimson'd drop by drop
The lichen, grit and boulders on
Bald old Braeriach's top,
We heard the bellowing of stags
Around Lord Berkeley's Seat,
And sniffed the bruised bog-myrtle that
We crushed beneath our feet.

We saw a rainbow round the sun
Above the Aonach Dubh,
Orange, green and indigo,
Red, violet and blue,
We heard a winter avalanche
Crash down from Corrie Odhar,
The croaking of a raven from
Ben Alder cottage door.

We smelt the smell of heather when
We burnt it for the tea,
And granite struck by granite at
The back of Corrie Fee,
We saw the twisted strata in
The glaciated lands,
The little specks of mica that
Stuck glistening in our hands.

We saw a grouse on Tolmount drag
What seemed a broken wing,
To lead us from her little ones
In tugged and twisted ling,

Sharp, shiny, shards of quartzite rock
Pure white among the peat,
And heard sad plovers whistle where
Canness and Isla meet.

Among the boulders of Broad Cairn
We saw the dawn of day
That grows on bare Mt Battock's back,
So cold and bleak and grey.
We heard the waters tumbling down
From Taggart's melting snow,
A roar that fades upon the wind
And comes and fades and goes.

We saw a sudden gleam of spate
In sun across the glen,
A dazzling ribbon in the mist
Which fades in mist again.
A salmon lying on a stone,
The Esk slid swirling by,
Then saw the ugly otter bite
That made the salmon die.

And there were many other things
Encountered near and far,
Exotic, strange, yet natural,
However much bizarre,
There's more to come far stranger, and
We hope you will be there
The day we hear the ptarmigan
Croak in the City Square.

See Edinburgh's, Aberdeen's,
And Glasgow's and Dundee's
Turn to a lichened wilderness
Of unpretentious screes,
And see the whole jing bang of life
Revert to what it was,
Obedient to the living God,
His judgment and his laws.

SYD SCROGGIE

AT LAST

They will bury you at last
When your Larig Gru is past
And you cannot hear it calling
On the Friday of the Fast,
When you cannot hear it calling
Though the waters tumble down,
Yet you cannot hear them falling
In the traffic of the town,
When you cannot hear them falling
At the lonely Pools of Dee,
And the golden Plovers calling
In the hubbub of Lochee,
When you cannot smell the heather
In the dingy Dundee weather,
And we cannot go together
To the Larig, you and me.
On the Friday of the Fast
When the summer sun is past
And the first, fine flakes are falling
They will bury you at last.

SYD SCROGGIE

BLOWS THE WIND TODAY

Blows the wind to-day, and the sun and the rain are flying,
  Blows the wind on the moors to-day and now,
Where about the graves of the martyrs the whaups are crying,
  My heart remembers how!

Grey recumbent tombs of the dead in desert places,
  Standing stones on the vacant wine-red moor,
Hills of sheep, and the howes of the silent vanished races,
  And winds, austere and pure:

Be it granted me to behold you again in dying,
  Hills of home! and to hear again the call;
Hear about the graves of the martyrs the peewees crying,
  And hear no more at all.

R. L. STEVENSON

Acknowledgements and Index of Authors

I am most grateful to all authors, publishers and other copyright holders who have given permission to use poems in this collection. In a very few cases copyright holders have been impossible to trace and, if their work has been used, it is with apologies and in the hope that such use will be welcomed. Readers are recommended to return to the source books mentioned; only a portion of the good things available could be included in this selection. Where a poet is out of copyright I have tried to note the most recent edition of his works as this may have a useful introduction or biographical notes. I am also much indebted to many people who sent material or suggestions or who helped trace authors and/or copyright, and also to the many editors of periodicals and the staffs of libraries who assisted in many ways. An anthology like this is very much a joint effort and as there are just too many to mention all, individually, please accept my warmest thanks now, collectively.

H.M.B.

The editor and publisher thank the following authors, copyright holders and publishers for permission to print copyright material. Where copyright no longer applies the names of poets and their poems are also included in alphabetical order.

ADDISON, William: Mrs Addison and Mrs Bulcraig, for 'Shadows Among the Ettrick Hills' from *Ettrick Verses* (1949)

ANGUS, Marion: 'Foxgloves and Snow' from *Selected Poems of Marion Angus* (1950)

ANNAND, J K and Macdonald Publishers, for 'Aince on the croun o Bidean', 'Lowpin owre a burn' and 'Man-muckle was I or I saw' from *Two Voices* (1968)

ANON: 'From the Lone Shieling', 'I leave tonight from Euston', 'Moorburn in Spring', 'The Old Munro Bagger', 'Said Maylard to Solly', 'Winter Climb'

BALL, Arthur and the *Scots Magazine*, for 'Above Ben Loyal' and 'The Tall Sky'

BARNETT, J Radcliffe: Mrs Janet Barnett, for stanzas from 'The Road that leads to Rannoch'

BARRIE, Hugh: Glasgow University, for lines, 'When I am dead . . .'

BATHGATE, Dave, for 'For Tony, Dougal, Mick, Bugs, Nick *et al*' and 'Rock Leader'

BELL, William, and Faber and Faber, for 'The Coolin Ridge', 'Elegy: On a Ledge of Rock He Lay' from *Mountains Beneath the Horizon*, 1950

BERRY, Martyn, for 'Cairngorm, November 1971'

BLACK, MacKnight, for 'Rock, Be My Dream'

BLACKIE, John Stuart, 'Why climb the mountains?', from *Lays of the Highlands and Islands*, and lines 'Now o'er the rugged peasants' cot'

BOWKER, Tom, for 'Eagle'

BROWN, George Mackay and The Hogarth Press Ltd, for 'Roads' from *Fishermen with Ploughs*

BROWN, Hamish and the *Scottish Mountaineering Club Journal*, for 'Aye there's hills, they say', 'Beyond Feith Buidhe', 'The bare soul will tramp', 'The Harlot' (from *Footloose Magazine*), 'In the Rut', 'Pitch Seven', 'Ronas Hill', 'Weather Rhymes', 'Wind' (from *Mountain Bothies Association Journal*); also in the *New Shetlander*, *Pennine Platform*, and *New Hope International*

BUCHAN, John: Lord Tweedsmuir and A P Watt Ltd, for lines from 'From the Pentlands' from *Poems Scots and English*

BUIST, A A: Mrs M E Buist and the Scots Magazine, for 'The Hills of God'

BURT, J F A, for 'Southward Bound', *S.M.C. Journal* (1933)

CAIRNCROSS, Thomas S: Mrs Finnie for lines from 'Grey Galloway'

CALDER, Dave, for 'At Kirk Yetholm'

CAMPBELL, Donald, for 'Hauf-Roads up Schiehallion', in *Scottish Poetry* 8 (Carcanet Press 1975)

CAMPBELL, Marion and Turnstone Press Ltd, for 'Levavi Oculos' from *Argyll, The Enchanted Heartland* (1977)

CHESTERTON, G K: A P Watt and Son on behalf of Miss D E Collins, and Methuen and Co, for 'Glencoe' from *Collected Poems* (1936)

CLOTHIER, Cal and *Akros*, for 'Soaring'

CONN, Stewart and Hutchinson and Co Ltd, for 'Marriage on a Mountain Ridge' from *An Ear to the Ground* (1972) and to *Akros*, for 'Under Creag Mhor' from *Thunder in the Air* (1967)

COXON, Philip, for 'April, Glengarry' from *Mountain Showers* (Dock Leaves)

190

CRAIG, David, for 'One Thousand Feet of Shadow' from *Homing*, Platform Poets (1980) and 'One Way Down' from *Latest News*, Journeyman Press (1978)

CRUICKSHANK, Helen B: Mrs Hunter and Gordon Wright Publishing for 'Caenlochan' and 'Schiehallion' from *Collected Poems* (1971)

CUTHBERTSON, D C: Alastair Cuthbertson, for 'A Picture' from *More Dream Roads* (1941)

DAUGHERTY, Michael and *Akros*, for 'Buzzard'

DAVIDSON, John: lines from 'The Testament of John Davidson' and lines from 'Winter in Strathearn'. *Poems of John Davidson* (Scottish Academic Press 1973)

DOBSON, A M and the *F.R.C.C. Journal*, for 'Bidean nam Bian'

DONALDSON, Islay Murray and the *Scots Magazine*, for 'Skye Summer'

DUTTON, G J F: the *S.M.C. Journal* and *Camp One* (Macdonald Publishing 1978), where most have appeared, for 'February Thaw', 'Hut', 'Magma', 'Of only a single poem'

ELIOT, T S: Faber and Faber, for 'Rannoch, by Glencoe' from *Collected Poems, 1909–1962*

FABER, Geoffrey: Faber and Faber, for 'St Mary's Loch' from *The Buried Stream*

FALCONER, Raymond and *Akros*, for 'No Voice of Man'

FERGUSON, Roy: Dan Ferguson, for 'The Island of Rhum' from *Once Familiar Ways* (Milfoil Publications)

FIRSOFF, Axel: Mrs L Firsoff, for 'The Spirit of the Cairngorms'

FRASER, Bárclay and *S.M.C. Journal*, for 'Mountain Days'

FRASER, Douglas J: 'Far in the West', 'Freedom of the Hills', 'Growing Old', 'Lost Leader', 'Mountain Vigil' 'On Looking at an Old Climbing Photograph', 'The Quiet Glen', 'The Spell of the Hills', 'To Alan', which have appeared in his collections *Landscape of Delight* (Macmillan Publishers) and *Treasures for Eyes to Hold* (The Lomond Press)

FRASER, Olive: Miss Norma Jeans and Miss Helena Shire for 'Benighted to the Foothills of the Cairngorms'

FULTON, Robin and Macdonald Publishers, for stanzas from 'A Cleared Land' from *Selected Poems* and for 'Stopping by Shadows' (Anvil Press)

GADSBY, Gordon, for 'The Lost Valley'

GARDNER, Alan and *Grampian Club Bulletin*, for 'On Walking Back to the Bus'

GARIOCH, Robert: Ian G Sutherland, Mrs Helen Willis and Macdonald Publishers, for 'Sisyphus' *from Collected Poems* (1977)

GAWSWORTH, John: Sidgwick and Jackson Ltd, for 'Skye' from *Collected Poems* (1948)

GIBSON, Wilfrid: Michael Gibson and Macmillan, London and Basingstoke, for 'Eagles and Isles', 'The Peak', and lines from 'Skye', from *Islands, Poems 1930–1932*

GILCHRIST, Alan, for 'Assynt'

GILLIES, Valerie and Canongate Publishing, for 'Clouds and Clay' from *Each Bright Eye* (1977)

GINGELL, David, for 'In Memoriam' and 'Older Now'

GLEN, Duncan and *Akros*, for part of 'Ane to Anither' from *Realities Poems* and 'Stanes' from *In Appearances*

GREIG, Andrew and Canongate Publishing Ltd, for 'On Falling' from *Men on Ice* (1977); for 'Marry the Lass?' from *White Boats* (Garret Arts)

HANNIGAN, Des for 'Ben Alder 1963–1977'

HARBORD, A M: 'At Euston' (*The Tatler & Bystander*)

HENDRIE, K G P: 'Beckon Me, Ye Cuillins' (*S.M.C. Journal* 1954)

HESKETH, Phoebe and *The Countryman*, for 'The Dipper' from *Lean Forward Spring* (1948)

HOLMES, W K: Blackie and Son Ltd, for 'The Old Mountaineer' and 'On the Heights' from *The Hills I Love* (1958)

HOPKINS, Gerard Manley: 'Inversnaid' (See *Poems of*, OUP 1975)

HUTCHISON, A G, for 'A'Chuilionn'

JACOB, Violet: John Murray Ltd, for 'The Gean Trees' and 'The Rowan', from *The Scottish Poems of Violet Jacob* (1945)

JEFFREY, William: Margaret W J Jeffrey for 'Glen Rosa' from *Selected Poems* (1951)

KEATS, John: 'Written Upon the Top of Ben Nevis'

KER, W P: Janet Adam Smith, for poems in her collection of Ker's *Birthday Poems for P.M.K.* (privately printed by AUP 1935); 'Theme and Variations' (in *S.M.C. Journal* and *Oxford Magazine*), 'There is Snowdrift on the Mountain' and 'A Song of Degrees' (in *Cairngorm Club Journal*)

LAMONT, Colin and *Akros*, for 'Rothiemurchus'

LANDLES, William and the *Scots Magazine*, for 'A Border Forecast' and 'On Ellson Fell'

LANG, Andrew: lines from 'Twilight on Tweed' (see *Poetical Works* 1923)

LINDSAY, Maurice and Paul Harris Publishing, for 'Highland Shooting Lodge' from *Collected Poems* (1979) and *Akros*, for 'In the Cheviots' from *This Business of Living*

MacCAIG, Norman and The Hogarth Press Ltd, for 'Above Inverkirkaig', 'High Up on Suilven', 'Moment Musical in Assynt', 'No Accident', 'One of the Many Days', 'Spate in Winter Midnight' from *Old Maps and New* (1978)

McDIARMID, Hugh: Mrs Valda Grieve and Martin Brian and O'Keeffe Ltd, for 'Scotland Small?' from the *Complete Poems 1920–1976*, edited by Michael Grieve and W R Aitken (1978)

McGAVIN, Stewart for 'Kythans'

MacGREGOR, Malcolm, for 'Rannoch Moor'

MACINTYRE, Duncan Ban: lines from the 'Last Farewell to the Hills'

MACKIE, Alastair and *Akros*, for 'Passin Ben Dorain' from *At the Heich Kirk-Yaird'*

MACLAGAN, Sir Douglas: 'The Battle of Glentilt'

MACLEAN, Alasdair: David Higham Associates and Victor Gollancz Ltd, for 'Death of a Hind', 'Envoy', and 'View from My Window' from *From the Wilderness* (1973)

MacLEAN, Sorley and Canongate Publishing, for 'Kinloch Ainort' from *Springtide and Neaptide, Selected Poems 1932–1972* and lines from 'The Cuillin' (William MacLellan)

MACMILLAN, James and Pettycur Publishing, for 'Hill Love', 'I like to think one day', 'Nightmare on Rhum' and 'What are you Thinking about?', from *Eye to the Hills* (1982)

McOWAN, Rennie and the *Scots Magazine*, for 'Highland Loves', 'The Hillman Looks Back', 'The Hooded Crow' (*M.B.A. Journal*), 'Mountaineering Bus', and 'The Things of the North'

MacPHAIL, Dougald: lines based on his Gaelic poem 'Island of Mull'

MACROW, Brenda G: the *Scots Magazine*, and Oliver and Boyd, for 'All Flesh is Grass', 'At the Shelter Stone', 'Climb in Torridon', 'In praise of Ben Avon', from *Unto the Hills* (1946) and *Hills and Glens* (1949)

MANN, Gill and *L.S.C.C. Journal*, for 'Mist'

MANSON, John and *Cencrastus*, for 'At a Ruined Croft'

MARSHALL, Matt: 'Wine o Living' from *The Travels of Tramp Royal* (William Blackwood 1932)

MICHAL, M L and *The Countryman*, for 'From Skye, Early Autumn'

MILBURN, Ken, for 'Motive for Mercy'

MILNE, J C: Mrs Milne and Aberdeen University Press, for 'Dolomites', 'Faur wid I dee?', 'Feels', 'The Lairig', 'The Patriot', from *Poems* (1976)

MITCHELL, Archie and *Cairngorm Club Journal*, for 'Hills of the Middle Distance'

MITCHISON, Naomi and Canongate Publishing, for 'The Boar of Badenoch and the Sow of Atholl', 'Buachaille Etive Mor and Buachaille Etive Beag', 'Wester Ross' from *The Cleansing of the Knife and Other Poems* (1978)

MONTGOMERIE, William and *The Adelphi*, for 'Stags' from *Via*

MORGAN, Edwin and Edinburgh University Press, for 'Canedolia' from *The Second Life* (1968)

MORLEY, David J, for 'Climbing Zero Gully'

MORRIS, Betty, for 'The Strath of Kildonan'

MUNRO, Neil: William Blackwood Ltd, for 'Nettles', from *The Poetry of Neil Munro* (1931)

MUNRO, Robin, for 'Apprentices' (*Sou' Wester*), 'Hills' (*Tribune*), 'Shetland, Hill Dawn' (*Akros*), and 'View' (*Akros*). (See *Shetland, Like the World* and *The Land of the Mind*, Dent)

MURRAY, Anne B and *L.S.C.C. Journal*, for 'Drumochter' and 'Then and Now'

MURRAY, Charles: The Executors of Charles Murray for 'Bennachie' and 'In Lythe Strathdon' from *Hamewith, The Complete Poems of Charles Murray*, Aberdeen University Press (1979)

NASH, Dorothy and *New Horizon*, for part of 'Kinloch' from *The Summer Sheiling and Other Poems* by Dorothy Nash and Lucy Taylor (1982)

NICHOLSON, Alexander: 'If you are a delicate man'

NISBET, Eilidh, for 'Three Girls on a Buttress' and 'To a Midge' (*L.S.C.C. Journal*)

OGILVIE, Will H: George and Wendy Ogilvie, for 'If I Were Old' from *The Land We Love* (Fraser, Dalbeattie 1910) and 'The Kingship of the Hills' from *A Clean Wind Blowing* (Constable 1930)

ORR, Christine: 'The Road' from *The Loud Speaker*. Also in *Punch* (1919) and *S.M.C. Journal*

OUSTON, Hugh and *Lines Review*, for 'The Climber surveys his Mountain'

PATEY, Tom: Mrs Elizabeth Patey and Victor Gollancz Ltd, for 'MacInnes's Mountain Patrol' and 'The Last of the Grand Old Masters' from *One Man's Mountains*

PILKINGTON, Lawrence: Lord Pilkington, for 'What called Me to the Heights?' from *Alpine Valley and Other Poems* (1924)

PRICE, Victor, for 'Highland Region' from *Two Parts Water*, Peterloo Poets

RAE, Hugh C and *Lines Review*, for 'Mountain Creed'

RAINE, Kathleen and George Allen and Unwin, for stanzas from 'Eileann Chanaidh' and 'The Wilderness' from *Collected Poems* (1981) and for 'Oreads' from *The Lost Country* (1971)

REDFERN, Roger, for 'Night Expedition from Ben Alder Cottage'

RICH, Vera, for 'Lion Gate' from *Heritage of Dreams* (1964)

RILEY, C L, for 'There are gods'

RIXSON, Denis, for 'Glen Pean' and *Chapman*, for 'The Ice Has Spoken'

ROBERTSON, Winifred: Messrs Strathern and Blair WS, for 'The Perfect Garden' (*L.S.C.C. Journal*, 1952)

SAUNDERS, Donald G and *Words*, for 'Ascent', the author, for 'On Fionaven'

SCROGGIE, Syd and David Winter and Son Ltd, Dundee, for 'Ante Mortem', 'At Last', 'Change and Immutability', 'The Drunken Dee', 'Loch Ossian', 'Long Ago', 'Poem 1972', 'The soot on the cassies', 'Space and Time', from *Give me the Hills* (1978)

SELKIRK, J B: Lines 'A Border Burn' (from 'Epistle to Tammus') from *The Complete Poems* (1932)

SHEPHERD, Nan: the literary executors and Messrs Edmonds and Ledingham, for 'The Hill Burns' and 'Images of Beauty' from *In the Cairngorms* (1934)

SMITH, Iain Crichton and Victor Gollancz Ltd, for lines from 'Deer on the High Hills—A Meditation' from *Selected Poems* (1970)

SMITH, Janet M, for 'Corries'

SMITH, Roger, for 'Lochan'

SMITH, W C: 'Coruisk'

SOUTAR, William: The Trustees of the National Library of Scotland for 'A Hint o' Snaw', 'Among High Hills', 'On the Hill', 'Owre the Hill', from *Collected Poems* (1948)

STEVENSON, R L: 'In the Highlands', 'Blows the Wind Today?'

STOTT, John G: 'The Scottish Mountaineering Club Song'

STRACHAN, Ian and the *Cairngorm Club Journal*, for 'The Silent Walls' and 'Silver in the Wind'

STUART, Alice V and H T Macpherson Ltd, for 'The Climbing Rope' from *The Door Between* (1963)

SYMMONS, Robert: the editor, *Isis*, for 'The Dam, Glen Garry'

TAYLOR, Lucy and Famedram Publishing, for 'Leac a' Chlarsair' from *Around Broadford, Poems from Skye* by Lucy Taylor, Lucy Key and Dorothy Nash

THOMAS, Edward: 'The Sheiling' (see *Edward Thomas: Collected Poems*, edited by R. G. Thomas, Oxford University Press, 1981)

THOMPSON, A R: 'Looking Down a Hill' from *Scottish Poetry* 7, University of Glasgow Press

TREMAYNE, Sydney and Chatto and Windus Ltd, for 'Discomfort in High Places' from *Selected and New Poems* (1973)

TULLOCH, Bill, for 'Beinn a' Ghlo' and 'NN 616410'

VALENTINE, G D: 'Night Up There', *S.M.C. Journal*

VOLWERK, Leen, for 'Bog' and 'Staoineag' (*M.B.A. Journal*)

WALLER, Janet, for 'Aviemore'

WATT, Lachlan MacLean: 'A Wind from the West' from *In Poets Corner* (1910)

WILL, James and *Cairngorm Club Journal*, for 'Mountain Sculpture'

WILSON, Elizabeth A and *Grampian Club Bulletin* for 'Snow Crystals on Meall Glas'

YOUNG, Andrew: Martin Secker and Warburg Ltd, for 'Dundonnel Mountains', 'The Eagle', 'The Echoing Cliff', 'The Falls of Glomach', 'Loch Luichart', 'Mist', 'The Paps of Jura' and 'Prospect of a Mountain' from *Complete Poems* (1974)

Index of First Lines

A company of mountains, an upthrust of mountains   117
A Gaelic bard they praise who in fourteen adjectives   111
A lizard fidgets in the sun   61
A mountain is a sort of music: theme   133
A small black wedge, the shepherd   47
Above Ben Loyal one wandering cloud   142
Above Stromness, the Hills of Hoy rise proud   142
Above the plains   14
Above the stream, grunting Staoineag stands   79
About us in white mist, ptarmigan   39
Ah, Tam! gie me a Border burn   51
Aince on the croun of Bidean   72
air was vibrant round the hills, The   114
Although you move among them as a friend   114
As I came o'er the Devil's Stair   161
As I strayed in the shade of the Buachaille   150
As the sun, its globe compressed in   67
At Kirk Yetholm   47
Auld Hamish knapped his whunstane chips   52
Awa te the hills, awa   161
Aye, there's hills, they say, rise tae the cloods   155

bare soul will tramp, The   175
Beckon me, ye Cuillins?   116
Before I crossed the sound   107
Ben Nevis is a mountain   80
bens camp by the road-side, The   66
Between the cloud and the ground   39
Black, crumbling rock. Dead scree. The dolorous wind   128
Blows the wind to-day, and the sun and the rain are flying   188
Body black in the rock spine of Quinag   137
Born in the purple the red grouse cry   11
Broom pods crackling in the heat   107
Bumpity doun in the corrie gaed whuddran the pitiless whun stane 162
But for a breathing-space the witch   115
But Sgurr nan Gillean the best Sgurr of them   119

Cannily/the mists smoor   38
Can one love a boulder   6
Cauld, cauld is Alnack   93
Caught on the shoulder of Beinn Mhor on a slope   123
Climbers are fools, forget   18
Corries are like pots of transmutation   73
Crouched up beneath a crowd of Grampian hills   96

197

dark is no more than a blanket, The   98
Do you remember that day of the roaring storm   169

Eagles and isles and uncompanioned peaks   29
Even the sky is the colour of copper   144

Far, far in the West   103
Far off, far off, so faint against the sky   171
Faur wid I dee?   184
Fecht for Britain? Hoot awa!   89
Few have seen the King Selkie and few the grand   84
Fin God made Buchan flat and gweed   98
Fingers aching, nails breaking   17
fleur has fa'en, The   41
From here, boulders are pebbles   182
From the lone shieling of the misty island   122
From year to year I shall return   175

Ghillies and shepherds are shouting Bravo   152
Give me my scallop shell of quiet: let me go   104
Glen Pean is in bright sunshine   112
Gulfs of blue air, two lochs like spectacles   134
Gyang over by Rothiemurchus when the snaw lies thick   100

Hae ye smelt the tang o heather   *10*
Half a mile from the shining sea   *26*
half-drying rocks in shades of gray   *36*
He hangs between his wings outspread   *29*
Here I stand   *18*
Here on the heich hill   *36*
Here the crow starves, here the patient stag   *67*
Here time unfastens knot and strap   *106*
Here it begins, the day we shall not forget   *70*
Here where the river is slender and small   *27*
Here where the wind skins Drumochter   *84*
High above Suilven an eagle soars   *135*
High, high and far away   *30*
High on Ben Alder on wintery night   *78*
High up, birches have a homely aspect   *102*
High up, I   *136*
hills are stark, their outlines hard with frost, The   *102*
Hills of the middle distance: crooked backs   *25*
Hillstones pebbles and boulders   *35*
hind, knocked sprawling by my shot, The   *33*
How can we justify a life   *13*

I came back to where we killed the deer   *77*
I came too late to the hills; they were swept bare   *43*
I climb the Barra half-hill   *124*
I found a garden of thyme and thrift   *172*
I have been in the hills all day   *167*
I have been there   *25*

I hope that Death is a pass   122
I like to think one day   184
I mind, when I dream at nicht   55
I never saw more frogs   62
I saw a herd of the wild red deer   88
I shall be quite content   178
I shall leave tonight from Euston   12
I stand on the deck of a small boat as rain sends   109
I thought the dawn would flush to sudden glory   42
I wandered up an autumn loaning   185
I watch, across the loch   132
I will attempt the Capel track   177
ice flow cut this valley, The   34
If I were old, a broken man and blind   52
If the mist comes down, just sit still   153
If you are a delicate man   120
Ill-advised, in these parts, to shout   126
Images of beauty and of destruction   98
I'm growin auld, I'm growing cauld   8
In loneliness or grief, I treasure yet my friendship with Ben A'an 92
In the highlands, in the country places   3
Island of Mull, island of joy   108
It is almost too simple   81
It is consummation, a mad rape   16
It is good to see the sunshine ebb on distant hills   101
It stands alone   105
It started with her shape on the map   131
It was a heat to melt the mountains in   77
I've aye been keen on the heich hills   56
I've had my share of mountain days in snow and rain and sun   149

Just for a handful of summits he left us   147

Larks trill in the quiet glen   26
Last night under the stars   33
last thing, the very, The   183
Leap in the smoke, immortal, free   53
Leaving the snows   94
Leisure hills, motorway connected.   44
Let us give thanks for the things of the north   128
Like most, one way or another, ours   138
Lost in the white world   59
Lowpin owre a burn   14

Mad in the midday sun I hae sclimed to the tap   56
Man-muckle was I or I saw   130
Many years back was an evening   174
Mine is the freedom of the tranquil hills   7
Mist—no sky   37
moon is down, The   42
More than people were cleared from these hills   141
mountains are dragons, The   110
mountain where I danced on moonlit stones, The   99

                                                                   199

No,/people are feared to fall off 19

No, our kind cannot live with these 125

Now o'er the rugged Peasants' cot 120

oa! hoy! awe! ba! mey! 163

O a' the isles o this braid sea 115

O' cam' ye here to hear a lilt 158

O far, fantastic line of notch and spire 122

O I gaed furth and far awa to see what I cou'd see 95

O sad for me Glen Aora 104

Oft on a dusky night of March, I've watched 31

Oh, long before the bere was steeped for malt 4

Oh, the big ice axe, it hangs on the wall 156

Older now 4

On a ledge of rock he lay 21

On Broad Cairn, I remember still 87

On Meall nan Con, the Peak of the Dogs 65

Once, in the burning age 50

Once more the miracle, still unexplained 168

Only a hundred yards, says Bob 79

Ower the grey sentinel hills 118

Out frae the wüd the gowk cries still 172

ptarmigan cries across the corries, The 27

Perched on a birch stump 28

Quoich, the Ey, the Slugain, The 91

Rain do not fall 37

Rain drifts forever in this place 127

Read me a lesson, Muse, and speak it loud 82

road moves on, melting, The 113

road that leads to Rannoch is the gangrel's royal way, The 62

road to the burn, The 143

Rock, be my dream 7

Said Maylard to Solly one day in Glen Brittle 121

Scotland small? Our multiform, our infinite Scotland small? 3

scourge of wind first, to flay, The 40

scree empties down the mountain, The 24

Seldom a simmer passed but him and me 91

Six children, dear God, died out in this waste 100

Skull stark 140

Skye rasps the mind. A tangle of harsh cries 117

slender pine skirts walls now silent, The 95

Slioch and Sgurr Mor 129

Slopping like sphagnum, battered, baptised in cloud, 41

Solway wind, The 49

soot on the cassies, The 9

So without sediment 96

star-crowned cliffs seem hinged upon the sky, The 68

Stranger with the pile of luggage proudly labelled for Portree 11

streams fall down and through the darkness beer, The   40
Stone and rock   127
Sullen Sullom Voe   144
summer pipers have flickered, The   32
sun was sinking when we reached the glen, The   24

tall sky fallen in the sea, The   141
There are always shadows among the hills   48
There are gods in this place   108
There are moments   60
There are some that love the Border-land and some the Lothians wide   85
There is no cut rock   83
There is snowdrift on the mountain, there is spindrift on the bay   58
There's no track   23
There's Tap o' Noth, the Buck, Ben Newe   90
They sucked at the sweat on his forehead   155
They will bury you at last   188
This darksome burn, horseback brown   58
This is not the way to die   21
Those two bad shepherds, hunched above their sheep   68
Though cuckoos call across the kyle   136
Through mist that sets the hills on fire   130
Three crests against the saffron sky   50
Today a wind from the West out over the hills came blowing   176
twinkling Earn, like a blade in the snow, The   54
Two things have set the world a-twist   89

Walking downhill from Suilven (a fine day, for once)   134
walls are down to window height, The   140
weather came down from Nevis, The   82
Wee strippit irritating beastie   154
We fluttered from the ridge   86
We lay upon the southern slope, and saw   121
We looked over the white sea   112
Well/we were hauf-roads up Schiehallion   76
We sailed in sunshine; but the glen was black   5
We saw the Brochan spectre from   186
We sit by the old tent   135
Wha gangs wi' us owre the hill   8
whale got my friend, The   181
What called me to the heights?   170
What hills are like the Ochil hills?   54
What is it that stirs the heart and mind   179
When I am dead   180
When I die   181
When I went up to Clova glen   88
When one climber fell to his doom, I also fell   20
When the days were still as deith   30
White gulls that sit and float   29
white shape is Loch Fionn, The   133
Why climb the mountains? I will tell you why   170
Winding, winding   69

wind is blowing harshly on the lake, The   48
Winter kept us in the valleys   126

years go by, and still both moor and mount, The   49
Years, long years ago, I read of a death I envied   74
Yesterday three deer stood at the roadside   64
Yestreen I stood on Ben Dorain, and paced its dark-grey path 63
You are not alone on the mountain   86
'You are old Munro bagger', the young man said   148
You led me to the hills   173
You've got halfway, and found it rather hard   15